It Happened In Series

IT HAPPENED ON THE
SANTA FE TRAIL

Steve Glassman

TWODOT®

GUILFORD, CONNECTICUT
HELENA, MONTANA
AN IMPRINT OF THE GLOBE PEQUOT PRESS

To my mother, Marguerite Glassman, a true plains settler

A · T W O D O T® · B O O K

Copyright © 2008 Morris Book Publishing, LLC

Text design by Nancy Freeborn
Map by M. A. Dubé © 2008 Morris Book Publishing, LLC
Front cover photo: The Santa Fe Trail in the Cristobal Mountains lithograph © CORBIS.
Back cover photograph: Santa Fe Fiesta, De Vargas Day," Santa Fe, New Mexico, cere-monies as they occurred in 1693, photo from 1921. Library of Congress. LC-USZ62-133424.

Library of Congress Cataloging-in-Publication Data is available on file.
ISBN 978-0-7627-4573-9

Printed in the United States of America
10 9 8 7 6 5 4 3 2 1

CONTENTS

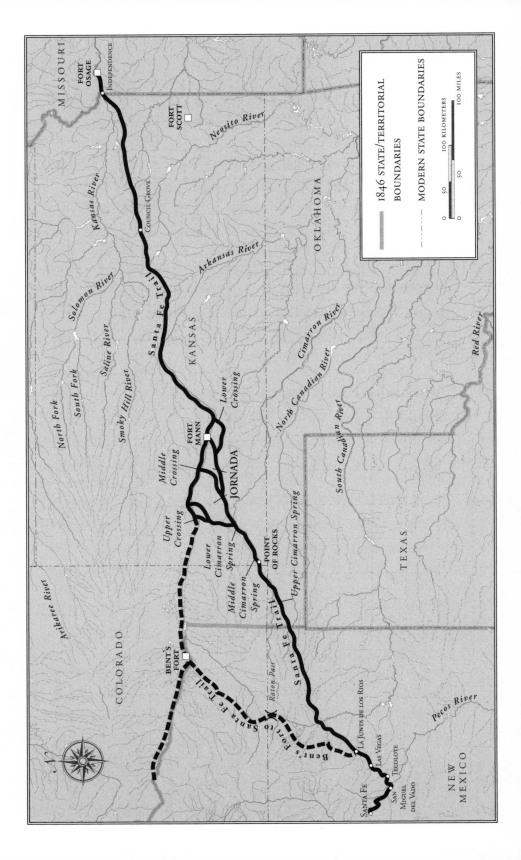

CONTENTS

INTRODUCTION

In the early years of the American West, three trails attained legendary status. They were, from the latest to the earliest, the Chisholm Trail, the Oregon Trail, and the Santa Fe Trail. The Chisholm "Trail," as spoken of today, was not really a trail in any ordinary sense of the word. A trace, it was laid out by a trader named Jesse Chisholm and ran from his store at present-day Wichita, Kansas, to another of his trading posts near Oklahoma City. Just before the end of the Civil War, Texas cattlemen, with herds of range-fattened steers, began pushing their cattle north to railroads being built west of Kansas City. They struck Chisholm's trace in central Okalahoma and followed it north, ending at the trailhead towns in Kansas. As different shipping points developed over a breadth of several hundred miles, the herders continued using the term Chisholm Trail for the path they followed, even though they may have no longer been following the original trace at all. The events that took place along this trail are often remembered today in television, movies, and books.

The other two trails were covered-wagon trails. In an important sense they were both "folk" trails, meaning they were developed without any important guidance from the government or big business. In the 1840s eastern families began heading west along the Platte River, following what would become known as the Oregon Trail, destined for the Willamette Valley. In 1843 more than a thousand pioneers moved west, and the migration had started in earnest. These settlers wanted what Americans have always wanted: good agricultural land where they could live without interference from civil or religious authorities. After a time some of the immigrants branched off and headed to California. In the late 1840s the Mormons used the eastern and central parts of the route on their mass migration to Utah. Therefore, this trail went by many names. Branches were called the California Trail or the Mormon Trail, which ran for the most part on the opposite side of the Platte River, and the whole thing was sometimes called the Overland Trail. About a half million people used it to move west before it effectively grew obsolete with the completion of the transcontinental railroad in 1869. The trail had many points of origin in Missouri, Iowa, and eastern Nebraska. It ran almost two thousand miles. Passage required about four months.

The Santa Fe Trail began two decades before the Oregon Trail. The impetus for it came from the persistent belief among Missouri frontiersmen that the people of New Mexico were eager for their cheaper American goods. The Spanish, however, desiring to protect their own trade, forbade American merchants from entering New Mexico.

In 1821, when word reached Missouri that the Mexicans had revolted against Spain, Missourians struck out across the plains to Santa Fe, the capital of New Mexico. While Captain William Becknell is credited with being the first to open the trade, in fact, two other parties of Missourians arrived in Santa Fe at almost the same time. But when Becknell drove wagons to Santa Fe the following year, he blazed a more dangerous but shorter road across the plains. All this made him the traditional "Father of the Santa Fe Trail."

Soon, however, professional traders recognized the potential of the New Mexican market. Adventurers like Becknell were shunted aside, even while many other Missourians were employed as teamsters, scouts, hunters, and the like. Becknell's party had set off from Franklin, Missouri, in the center of the state, but for most of the trail's long history, the Kansas City area would serve as the jumping-off place. (Many of those braving the Overland Trail also started here.)

From Kansas City to Santa Fe was about 750 miles going the shortest distance across the Cimarron route, and a bit over 800 miles on the longer but safer branch through a pass in the Rocky Mountains. This so-called mountain route was opened for wagon travel in the 1840s. Wagon trains crept along at about fifteen miles a day. The entire trip took about six weeks.

Some wagons were drawn by mules. Others were pulled by oxen. Mule skinners rode the animal in front of the left fore wheel of the wagon. Bull whackers, the name for ox-train drivers, walked beside their charges. Both mule skinners and bull whackers controlled their animals by the use of whips. They would snap on one side or the other to guide the animals. Contrary to popular images, reins were not used, and there were no seats in the front of the huge freight wagons. The average large freight wagon carried about six-thousand pounds of goods. Toward the end of the trail era, many wagons pulled a smaller wagon behind, called a trailer.

To an extent trail hands lived off the land. Their packed provisions typically consisted of something like fifty pounds of flour, the same amount of bacon, ten pounds of coffee, and twenty of sugar per man. But buffalo and other game supplied most of the meat. Occasionally, beans, dried fruit, and crackers were also taken, but these "luxuries" were considered dispensable. "Bread" was made by mixing bacon grease and flour. Salaterus (or baking soda) was added if available. Sometimes a powder obtained from the white residue left after a buffalo wallow or other body of water had dried was substituted. The batter was fried over a fire of whatever fuel was at hand. Often on the prairie this meant buffalo chips (dried buffalo droppings).

After the Civil War the trail became progressively shorter. As the railroad traveled west out of Kansas City, the trail began wherever the tracks stopped. In 1880 the railroad reached Santa Fe, and the longest serving of the Old West trails became history. Today Interstate 70 parallels the route of the railroad west of Kansas City, and Interstate 25 follows the old trail through the mountain passes to Santa Fe. U.S. Highway 56 runs fairly close to the Cimarron route, and U.S. Highway 50 follows the mountain route, until it meets I-25.

The importance in American history of these two covered-wagon trails, the Oregon and the Sante Fe, can hardly be overemphasized. Thanks to them, eastern America penetrated—and ultimately claimed—the West. Although the early territory of Oregon was jointly administered by Britain and the United States, American covered-wagon immigrants, by their sheer numbers, settled the question of which country would finally own this territory. Similarly, the number of American gold prospectors, arriving mainly by the Overland and Santa Fe Trails, overwhelmed the very small indigenous population of California. Few Americans actually took up residence in New Mexico, but the trail showed the local folks that relations with the United States were to their advantage. After the Mexican-American War (1846–1848), New Mexico territory, as well as much of the Southwest (including California), was incorporated into the United States with relatively minimal opposition from the local inhabitants.

Many of the enduring images we have of the Old West were forged along the Santa Fe Trail. Some wagon trains became lost in the so-called Cimarron Desert in southwest Kansas. One such, supposedly, cut the ears of their mules and drank their blood. Fortunately, they found pools of alkali-laden water in the Cimarron River and averted disaster. The trail passed through the hunting grounds of some of the most famous Indian tribes of the West. The Comanche, the Kiowa, the Pawnee, the Cheyenne, and the Arapaho all raided and skirmished, at one time or another, along the trail.

Many of these stirring episodes are included here in this slim volume. Read them. Enjoy them, and keep in mind the larger historical context—namely, that the Santa Fe Trail helped incorporate the Southwest into the United States of America.

THE LAST CONQUISTADOR
ON THE SANTA FE TRAIL

- 1601 -

IT WAS JUST AS HIS APACHE GUIDE HAD PROMISED. There ahead on a sandy plain in the land that would one day be known as Kansas, Juan de Oñate spied a village of conical grass huts built by the Quivira Indians. Don Juan held up his hand, signaling the caravan to halt. The word passed back like the jerking movements of a caterpillar. The nine large-wheeled oxcarts, the seventy officers, the various servants, and even the Apache tribesmen who had attached themselves to Don Juan's expedition, all stumbled to a halt.

After studying the situation, Don Juan ordered his fighting men into full regalia. They rode to their carts, dismounted, and let their servants garb them in coats of mail and iron-visored helmets. Other retainers buckled armor to the horses. Within two years these soldiers would all become noblemen. The Apaches, longtime enemies of the Quivira, danced with glee. But with a gesture Don Juan ordered all Apaches far to the rear. His order was reinforced by the vicious looks of the seventy men donning their armor. The Apaches reluctantly moved to the back.

And then Don Juan did a strange thing. He instructed his majordomo to open his leather trunk. Don Juan donned a velvet jacket with a ruffed collar. He put on a pair of intricately woven tights and a flowing Chinese taffeta cape. He shod his feet in cordovan slippers. On his head went a luxuriant floppy hat more suitable for an audience with a king than for a battle, which was exactly the point. Don Juan was betting his fortunes on this expedition, and so a successful interview with the Quivirans was essential.

As Don Juan urged his horse toward the distant ranks of warriors, he could see why these people called themselves the Kitkitish. He'd been told by his Aztec guide, Jusepe, that the word meant "raccoon eyes." The warriors, thrusting their spears into the air and dancing excitedly, had masks tattooed around their eyes. Some of the men were throwing handfuls of dirt up in the air, the sign on the southern plains for war.

But the story of the most important early caravan on what was to become the Santa Fe Trail actually started with Juan's father. When Cristobal de Oñate arrived in Mexico in 1534, Cortez had already defeated the Aztecs and had secured the central Mexican highlands. Cristobal soon set about making his fortune as a bureaucrat, ending up with one-fourth interest in what may have been the richest silver strike in the world.

His son Juan wanted to use this fortune to develop a new colony to the north of Mexico. But first he had to gain the king's approval. This meant convincing the Council of the Indies and King Carlos that he was the best man for the job. Juan promised to provide two hundred soldiers for the expedition into the area called New Mexico, agreeing to support these men and their families and the enormous baggage train necessary to maintain them. Naturally, Juan made similar arrangements with many of his followers, that is that they would provide for the people in their entourages out of their own pockets. In return, Juan promised them estates or shares of the supposed riches of the new province. Others were enticed along with the lure of rising to nobility, the *hidalgo,* even if only in the lower ranks. Five years' service in the new colony allowed one to prefix his name with the title of don. As a bonus, a noble could not be jailed for debt.

Juan gained the appointment in 1595. He assembled his company on the frontier of what we now call Chihuahua, Mexico. Then he waited for the final word from Madrid. He waited . . . and waited . . . and waited. Probably no truer test of his leadership could have been devised than for him to keep his expedition intact in the wilderness for more than two and a half years. Finally, in January 1598, the order to move out came. Numbering more than five hundred men, Juan's expedition set off across the Concho River, crossing it in flood. Included in the train were a half dozen shaved-head Franciscan monks.

On the march Juan's expedition strung out for two miles. It took a full hour to pass any given location. By early summer the giant caravan had crawled into the southern reaches of the Pueblo dwellers along the Rio Grande in present-day New Mexico. While the Pueblo Indians hailed from many linguistic and ethnic stocks, all adopted a similar culture. That culture included living in fortified multiroom dwellings, practicing irrigated agriculture, and manufacturing highly ornamental clay pots. After the march through the desert with an army of hungry followers, Juan was interested in these Pueblo dwellers as much for their stored grains as for their silver. But he received nothing.

The inhabitants fled before the soldiers, stripping their corncribs bare as they left. The Puebloans already knew of the Spanish by earlier ill-intentioned expeditions into their land. These expeditions sometimes kidnapped Puebloans to use as slaves in the mines, making the Indians very wary. It wasn't until Juan approached present-day Albuquerque that he and his entourage were greeted enthusiastically. They were put up in a room that appeared to have been specially prepared for them. Part of the preparations included freshly white-washed walls. But when the walls dried, the dim outline of a mural showed the Indians sacrificing a party of monks. Juan had heard of this expedition that had disappeared into the country some years before. After a one-night stay Juan hastily moved his expedition on.

As he traveled, Juan claimed the entire territory of New Mexico in the name of the king. He put his company up in winter quarters near present-day Santa Fe. While the monks set about converting the Indians to Christianity, his minions scouted for the precious metals everyone confidently expected the territory to yield. But almost none was found. What the Spaniards did get was cold. The mountains where they founded their colonies were almost a mile and a half above sea level. Winters were dismally frigid, and summers yielded little in the way of food. "Corn is God," a monk in Juan's entourage wrote.

Other troubles beset Juan's colonists as well. Before a year in the new colony had passed, the inhabitants of Acoma Pueblo had risen up against their new overlords. After three years of deprivation and no riches, even Juan's Spanish retainers began to threaten mutiny. Juan had to show a success. At first he planned a march to the Sea of Cortez, which he erroneously believed to be the Pacific. But then he chose instead to head toward the long-fabled land of Quivira, visited by Coronado in 1541. He hoped to find there that which had eluded at least two earlier Spanish expeditions: the Seven Cities of Cibola.

Roughly following what would become, centuries later, the Santa Fe Trail, Juan's caravan dipped south out of the Santa Fe valley and through Galisteo Pass. When he hit the Canadian River, he went east, paralleling (but a bit south of) the road American teamsters would blaze 220 years later. When mired in some sand hills in eastern Texas, he corrected his course northward, crossing the Cimarron and then the Arkansas Rivers. The vast, almost-flat plain intimidated even the fearless Spanish. One soldier remarked that they felt as insignificant as ants in a bowl.

Here they discovered vast herds of buffalo, which they called cibola. To the undernourished conquistadors the meat was a godsend. They glutted themselves on buffalo steaks and hump roasts. Then they came on the miserable teepee village of the Escanjaques. Some modern scholars think they may have been a Siouian or perhaps Caddoan tribe, but long called a band of Plains Apache, these folk gleefully guided the Spanish to their more prosperous neighbors. Called the Quivira by the Spanish, they were the Escanjaques' longtime enemies, and the very people Juan was hoping to find, and now the two groups stood face-to-face.

The line of armor-clad soldiers clanked to within arrow shot of the assembled Quivira warriors. Juan de Oñate in his court finery rode in the lead. The Aztec, Jusepe, went ahead. He had accompanied the Bonilla and Humana expedition into the country fifteen years before and knew how to communicate with the Quiviran people by sign language. More importantly, he bore gifts of manufactured cloth, glass beads, and iron products. The Quivirans received the gifts. They put down their arms. Don Juan rode forward and fastened a pendant around the leader's neck. Don Juan professed friendship with the Quivira. He told them that they were now under the protection of the Spanish king. To show the power of the Spanish, Don Juan ordered a mail-clad soldier to dismount. He offered to let tribesmen fire arrows at him. The two best archers in the tribe came forward. One aimed at the face, the other the heart. They unleashed a half dozen arrows, firing almost as fast as a Colt revolver. But the flint-headed arrows shattered on the Spaniard's visor and breastplates.

Then Don Juan summoned a squadron of soldiers from their horses. They shouldered their harquebuses. These guns resembled miniature, shoulder-fired artillery pieces. They had to be steadied by a forked rest. A thunderous volley of lightning bolts cut loose, and when the voluminous, sulfur-stinking smoke cleared, the target had all but disappeared. The tribesmen were awed. The Spanish, for their part, were also impressed by these Quivirans, which modern anthropologists have identified as the Wichita. A bit shorter, heavier, and darker than the Indians of the Southwest, these people were physically attractive, even if their chest and arms, as well as their eyes, were tattooed. Their homes were well kept. In warm weather they lived in shelters like lean-tos. In cold weather they resorted to large beehive-shaped grass houses, thatched with bundles of the tall bluestem that grew on the prairie bottoms. The flatlands on the far side of the Arkansas seemed one long village. All told, the Quivira numbered about thirty thousand.

None of this astonished the Spaniards as much as the Indians' vast cornfields. Growing among the rows of corn were beans and various squashes. And these products were dried, placed in animal-skin bags, and stored in underground caches. Dried buffalo meat was also kept in this way. These food stores provided for the Kitkitish in hard times. The crops not needed for their own consumption were dried and traded to other tribes. Among the treasures found in the chiefs' lodges were turquoise and fine pottery from the Southwest, excellent bows made from the bois d'arc tree of northeast Texas, and a few copper ornaments.

While his men gorged themselves on Quiviran vegetables and meat, Juan questioned the leaders closely. The gold he sought was not to be found, but some of the trade goods he saw gave him hope.

Many of the Quivirans adorned themselves with seashells, despite the fact that the South Seas (Pacific Ocean) and the Oceano Atlantico lay a long way off. Don Juan allowed himself to hope that the fabled Northwest Passage was close at hand. It was common (but mistaken) knowledge that the English pirate Francis Drake had returned to Britain by this passage. If Juan could find that sea route, he could shift his colony to the fruitful lands of Quivira. He could be supplied directly from Spain. All this would allow him his greatest hope, which was for New Mexico to become a country unto itself and not just a mere dependency of Mexico. Had his dream borne out, he would then have become known as the Father of North America.

But as we know, Quivira was located in the very heart of North America, and the Northwest Passage was an illusion. Neither Juan, Francis Drake, nor anyone else ever found it. Juan's expedition retreated to the nutrition-starved mountains of New Mexico. He vowed to seek the passage again, but there is no record that he did so. He hung on in New Mexico for almost a decade more, quelling uprisings and fighting off Apache and Navajo attacks. Deserters filtered south, giving dire testimony of goings-on in the province. Finally, in 1610, Juan was recalled. He was summoned before a royal court of inquiry and found guilty of using excess force when putting down Pueblo rebellions and unjustly executing four men, two Indian and two Spanish. His punishment amounted to a fine of six thousand ducats and an order never to return to New Mexico. He traveled to Spain hoping for a reversal of the verdict. Ultimately, Juan was officially pardoned. The money for the fine was returned to him, but the order to stay out of New Mexico was never lifted. In 1630, before Juan was able to come back to the New World, he died of a heart attack, some would say a broken heart.

Coronado's expedition, fifty years before Juan's, had accomplished little from the point of view of the Spanish colonists. It had even been forgotten about by the Spaniards in Mexico. Today historians, however, appreciate the information he provided, and Coronado's name is known to every American as the great explorer of the Southwest. Juan de Oñate, on the other hand, left a small but flourishing colony of Euro-Americans in New Mexico. That colony has maintained itself to this very day. Even though Juan sometimes treated the Indians harshly, many of the communities that Juan swore to protect are still in place and carrying on. Contrast that with Indian tribes in other parts of the United States. Almost all have either completely disappeared or been pushed from their ancestral homes.

In terms of the Santa Fe Trail, Juan opened the southern extension, known as the Camino Real. This was the road that ran from Santa Fe to Chihuahua and points south. Many of the goods shipped later from the United States to the Southwest on the Santa Fe Trail ended up going down this trail. Those areas had much silver and also a need for cheaper American products. Regarding the Santa Fe Trail itself, Juan, like Coronado, was probably just following a route long used by Indian traders. The trade goods that Juan should have paid attention to were the copper ornaments of the Quiviras. They had probably originated in the Great Lakes area. Traders plying the Missouri River had probably brought them overland from the closest point on that river to Quivira. Many years later, Santa Fe wagoners would ply the same route on their way to Santa Fe.

NATHAN BOONE DISCOVERS
A SALT SPRING

- 1804 -

THE YOUTH IN THE LEATHER HUNTING SHIRT and felt hat bore a remarkable resemblance to John Wayne. Though only twenty-two, he had already made a small fortune (eight hundred dollars) the previous winter. He and his companion had trapped nine hundred beavers. Their base camp was near where the Wakarusa flowed into the Kansas River, just a few miles from where the Santa Fe Trail would pass twenty years later. The young man's name was Nathan Boone. He was the youngest son of famous frontiersman, Daniel Boone. It was no surprise that he would be a fine woodsman. But right now, Nathan Boone was scared to death.

Twenty fierce-looking fellows had just popped into view. They wore loincloths and moccasins with leggings. Although it was late November, only one old man wore a buffalo robe over his shoulders, and the rest had not a stitch above the waist. Their heads were plucked bald except for a fantastic scalp lock, which was braided with feathers and ornaments. They were tall, handsome fellows, probably Osage. Back in the settlements, the Osage were considered friendly to whites. But Nathan wasn't in the settlements. Nathan was trespassing on Osage lands. He knew that he was at the Indians' mercy.

The leader called to Nathan. Nathan had trapped this area for the past several winters but had never actually seen an Indian away from the settled areas before. His father on a long hunt hereabouts had been discovered by a party of Osage. Luckily for him, it had begun to snow. The snow hid camp. Daniel tunneled under a snowbank. He stayed in that lair for days before the Osage gave up and went on their way.

"What should we do, Nathan?" his partner, Matthias, asked.

"Dismount," Nathan advised, as he slowly got off his horse. "Take your shooting iron. Go very slow. We don't want to provoke them."

As the two parties of men met, the Indians surrounded the young trappers. Two Osage warriors wrested the reins of the saddle horses from Nathan and Matthias. Concentrating on keeping a tight grip on their rifles, the young white men let the reins slide through their fingers. Other Indians removed the bale of furs from the packhorse. They spread the fifty-six beaver and twenty-two otter hides on the ground.

"Where did you get these?" the Indian spokesman wanted to know.

Not willing to give up the fruits of his trapping efforts, Nathan told a fib. He said he and Matthias were working for the Chouteau trading house in Saint Louis. The name Chouteau made the leader take notice. Nathan pointed to the traps dangling from the pack saddle. He showed them the Chouteau markings on the iron implements. A look of puzzlement came over the leader's face. The Chouteau were the first family of Saint Louis, and the good friends of the Osage. He would not want to annoy them. "That just means you rent those traps from the Chouteaus, maybe," the Indian said, after a pause. Then with a nod, he made up his mind against Nathan and his friend. He ordered his warriors to round up the horses, furs, and anything else his companions wanted.

As the band of Osage departed, the leader warned the two white men, "Clear out. There are more Indians in these woods looking for you. They may not treat you as well as we did."

Not long after the first party disappeared, a second group spotted the trappers. They beckoned to the whites. Nathan and Matthias took to their heels. They ran into thick cover along the riverbank, then slunk along for another ten miles before making camp. The next morning, being extremely hungry, they shot a deer. But the second group of Indians were still looking for Nathan and Matthias. The crack of the rifle alerted them to the young trappers' presence. Four Indians came into camp, two on horseback and two on foot. Seeing nothing of value except the guns, they demanded Nathan and Matthias surrender their weapons. The Indians even grabbed for their rifles. But the young men were determined not to let them go. They wrestled with the Indians, hanging on as though for dear life, which they believed the loss of their weapons would probably cost them. Finally, they struck a compromise. Nathan and Matthias gave the Indians their heavy blanket coats and a roasted haunch of venison. They kept their guns.

After consuming their fill, the Indians, who said they were Sac, insisted the young white men come with them. Having no alternative, the boys did as instructed. They refused to walk in front as they Indians wanted, fearing they would be shot. The Sac were the enemies of everyone, the Osage and white men alike. In fact, it was widely (and correctly) believed that the Sac were allies with the British. Expecting the worst, Nathan told Matthias under his breath that if the Indians gave any indication of violence, to shoot the man on the horse nearest him. Nathan would pot the other one. Then each trapper, with his hunting knife, would stab the Indian closest to him. They marched tensely side by side for a time, and then two more Indians joined their group. Their plan would no longer work.

It was clear that things were coming to a head when the Indians halted. They clumped together for a conference. Then one of them marched sternly to Nathan. With the ramrod of his rifle, he struck Nathan in the face. Though reeling from the force of the blow, Nathan commanded Matthias not to fire. The two whites and six Indians glared at each other. Then the Indians demanded the whites leave. Nathan shook his head. He told the Indians to go first. The Indians refused. Each side was certain the other would fire on their fleeing forms. So they struck a bargain. The whites would give each warrior some powder, shot, and flints, and then the Indians would depart.

After each native had received his share from the trappers, the supposed Sac (who were probably Osage) backed out of sight.

Once the Indians could no longer be seen, the two trappers broke into a dead run. They ran until nightfall when they made camp in a cave without a fire—or food. Little did they know their ordeal was just beginning. The next morning Nathan shot a turkey, and they roasted the bird over a small fire. Snowflakes began to fall. Then it turned cold, very cold. It was so cold their guns could not be sighted accurately. The men had only five rifle balls between them, and each shot at a potential meal missed. Snow continued to fall until it was knee deep. The men struggled along the Missouri River in the bitter cold. They cut up one of the ramrods of their guns to use the pieces for bullets, but these wood bullets proved worthless. At long last they found a tree that had been used for target practice. They dug five flattened shot from the timber. Over a fire they softened the bullets and reshaped them.

Good thing, too. Shortly thereafter, they found some abandoned

Osage lodges. In one of the shelters, a panther crouched, ready to pounce. Nathan's shot killed the big feline. While Matthias roasted the meat, Nathan made two vests from the skin. Nathan later said the meat tasted mighty "sweet and cattish." After several more days of tramping through the snow, they spotted a lone set of footprints. Indian or white hunter, the men followed the tracks ready to throw themselves on the mercy of whomever they encountered. The footprints led to a camp of white hunters, friends and relatives of the two young men. They were saved.

Nathan's wife, Olive, later joked that she had the Osage to thank for Nathan's being home for Christmas that year. It was the first Christmas they had spent together since their wedding. Poor Matthias, on the other hand, never recovered from the awful cold and fright. He took to a sickbed where he remained for a couple years before dying.

But the men had made an accidental discovery on their trek that would change the course of Nathan's life, as well as American history. Nathan noticed a small stream entering the Missouri's north bank on their return journey. It wasn't frozen. Tasting it, Nathan found it salty. Salt was an extremely valuable commodity on the frontier. It was used to give food taste and preserve meat. A bushel of salt was worth as much as $2.50.

Nathan noted his discovery, and a few months later led a pack train west from near St. Louis. His older brother, Daniel Morgan Boone, and a crew of men accompanied him. Their packhorses were burdened by large iron kettles. When reaching the salt spring, Nathan set some of the men to chopping firewood. Others constructed a foundation of limestone on which the kettles would boil brine. Once they were properly set up, the brothers produced as much as twenty-five bushels of salt a day. The potential profits were enormous.

But the work was hot and sweaty. Three hundred gallons of brine were required to produce one bushel of salt. It was not really suited to Nathan and Daniel Morgan's temperament. They were frontiersmen, not businessmen. By 1808 the brothers had leased the saltworks for approximately one hundred dollars a month. But Indian troubles may have prevented the brothers from receiving their payments. By 1811 the boys had sold their interest to two brothers named James and Jesse Morrison.

Though not profitable in terms of money, the Boones' adventures had laid the foundation for the settlement of central Missouri. The spring became known as Booneslick, and the road they blazed was called Booneslick Trace, now being considered for a national historical trail. The saltworks they started continued to be one of the few commercial enterprises in the area. It was a place where a little ready money could be made. Most importantly, all of this led to the establishment of Franklin, Missouri, just eight miles away. It was from Franklin that the first traders, many of whom had earlier labored in the saltworks, headed off to Santa Fe.

AN ARISTOCRAT'S BAD LUCK

- 1817 -

BY ANY STANDARD AUGUST PIERRE CHOUTEAU WAS frontier aristocracy. His grandfather had founded Saint Louis, Missouri. The capital of South Dakota is named for his brother, Pierre (a fur-trading and railroad magnate, and one of the richest men in the United States). His brothers Cyprian and Liguest traded with Indians out of a log cabin on the future site of Kansas City, Missouri, years before anyone else inhabited the spot. August Pierre, who went by his initials A. P., was highly educated too, speaking several languages and having graduated from West Point.

In May of 1817 the governor of New Mexico found his company enjoyable. The governor liked August Pierre's manners so well that he sent soldiers to fetch him to the governor's mansion from the jail cell where he was being kept for trespassing on New Mexican territory.

A. P. was not nearly as fond of the governor.

With many a flourish the governor went on and on in his office about what a fine fellow he, the governor, was. He mentioned (once again) all the wonderful things he had done for A. P. He told A. P. that he was much more generous than most any other governor would have been.

A. P. stared glumly into the clay cup of water the governor had so generously given him. He warned himself, *Don't say it.*

Then the governor said, "What more could you want of me?"

And A. P., in spite of himself, could not keep from blurting out, "My liberty, Mr. Governor."

At that, the governor called, "Sergeant. Come. Take this miserable American swine back to the guardhouse."

A. P. was unceremoniously escorted back to his dungeonlike cell.

What had one of the most socially eligible men in the West done to get himself locked up in a Santa Fe prison? Along with his cousin Jules DeMun, he had tried to open the Santa Fe Trail. Their problem was that they had attempted this feat a few years too early. The Spanish still controlled Mexico and refused to let foreigners do business in their territories.

In 1815 he and DeMun had outfitted a forty-five-man expedition to the headwaters of the Arkansas River. This was a little more than a decade after the United States had acquired Louisiana, and the boundaries of the territory were not yet clear. The Spanish authorities warned these French-speaking Americans they were on land claimed by the Crown. A. P. nevertheless managed to pack out forty-four panniers of furs, blazing what in later days would come to be called the mountain route of the Santa Fe Trail. Shortly after crossing what is now the western border of Kansas, A. P.'s party was set upon by more than 150 Pawnee Indians. A. P. and his men were trapped on an island in the Arkansas River. The men used the packs of furs for barricades. One French trapper was killed and three were wounded. Seven Pawnees died in the battle. "Chouteau's Island," west of Lakin, Kansas, has remained in trail lore even though the island has long since eroded away.

At the mouth of the Kansas River, he loaded his furs onto a barge, then returned to the upper Arkansas. In the meantime partner DeMun had continued to cultivate the Spanish authorities in Santa Fe. It didn't help. There were rumors that DeMun and A. P. had built a fort on the Arkansas River. Two hundred Spanish soldiers escorted DeMun to the river, looking for the fort. But not finding anything, they released DeMun. He and Chouteau were once again warned to get out of the disputed territory. Being slow learners, they hung around, had their goods confiscated, and were kept prisoner for about six weeks. They arrived in Saint Louis penniless, figuring they had lost $30,000 worth of furs and equipment (about $500,000 in today's dollars).

The rest of A. P.'s life did not go much better than the expedition to the Southwest. Borrowing money, he opened a store in Saint Louis. It went bust. He retired to the lower Arkansas River in present-day Oklahoma and commenced trading with the Osage and other prairie tribes. He also dealt with eastern Indians, such as the Kickapoo, who were moving into the Indian Territory. At first it appeared he had hit pay dirt. Receipts for 1825 show fifty thousand pounds of deer skins, four hundred pounds of beaver, sixty bear pelts, and a miscellaneous assortment of other furs, all worth a gross total of $17,500. A. P. and his partner received a clear profit of about a thousand dollars each. He looked forward to the arrival of the Creeks and Cherokees, figuring they would provide even more trade. They had been promised a lot of money for moving to Oklahoma. The displaced tribes arrived. But their support funds did not.

A. P. helped the impoverished Creeks, lending them more than $5,000 worth of food, clothes, and hardware. But he then made a claim against government payments to the Creek Indians. Was his motivation that of Indian benefactor or shrewd businessman? Payments made by the U.S. government to foreign "nations," native or otherwise, were considered plums ripe for the plucking by frontier businessmen. Of the $5 million the United States paid Spain for Florida, every cent settled claims of Georgia planters for runaway slaves. A fair amount of the gold in the Chouteau family coffers in Saint Louis had come from just such payments. Nevertheless, A. P.'s Indian clients trusted him.

A. P.'s influence within the Indian Territory was enormous. He spent the last dozen years of his life mediating disputes between tribes. The ingredients for major catastrophes were in place, such as when the Cherokee were given lands already occupied by the Osage. A. P. had much to do with settling these problems more or less peacefully. He talked the prairie tribes into agreeing to allow the eastern Indians to hunt buffalo on the plains. Due in part to A. P.'s influence, the Osage began trading with the Comanche, goods for horses, rather than raiding.

On a Christmas day in 1838, twenty-one years after he was clapped in prison in New Mexico, A. P. died at his trading post in Oklahoma. Without his influence the Santa Fe Trail would have been even more dangerous than it was. "Colonel" A. P. Chouteau was interred with full military honors by his soldier friends at nearby Fort Gibson, Oklahoma. Josiah Gregg, Santa Fe trader and trail historian, tells us that great was the Indians' grief when they were informed "that their favorite trader had died."

CAPTAIN WILLIAM BECKNELL
CAN'T FIND THE COMANCHE

- 1821 -

WITH SNOW FLURRIES SWIRLING ABOUT, Captain William Becknell led his five men up through a mountain pass in what is now south central Colorado. When their horses, worn down by cold and exhaustion, could go no farther, Captain Becknell ordered his men to dismount. He told some of them to take the horses to what shelter could be found. Others he commanded to follow his lead. He commenced pulling at rocks, piling some of the stones to the side and rolling others down the slope. The men worked all of one day, rested fitfully in the cold that night, and then continued moving rocks the next morning.

When a crude trail had been cleared to the top of the cliff, the men led their animals (loaded with precious trade goods) along the rudely sculpted way. At one point a packhorse slipped. No amount of pulling on the frightened animal's halter rope could save it. The horse plunged over the side, crashing into the canyon below. After a frightful amount of terrified neighing, a shot from one of the men's rifles put it out of its misery.

Leaving the men no time to dwell on the horse's dreary fate, Becknell ordered them to shake a leg. It was late in the season. They had to get out of the mountains before the winter's snows caught them. All five of the men did as he commanded. They put their backs into the job. When they finally made it over the crest of the pass, below lay New Mexico.

If Becknell and his men weren't careful, their fates might be no better than that of the horse that fell into the canyon. Or they could follow the example set by Robert McKnight nine years before. After learning of a rebellion against Spanish authority by a Father Hidalgo (and not knowing that the revolution had failed), McKnight had traveled to Santa Fe only to be jailed by the Spaniards. He spent nine years in prison.

For two weeks Becknell's company pressed south and west across the plains. Their horses were so worn out that they only traveled eight to fifteen miles a day. Food for the men was almost gone. Other than a bighorn sheep they had killed near the pass, even game was hard to come by. One night they had to make camp without water or wood for a fire. The wind whistled out of the northwest. It snowed some. Then on the morning of the thirteenth of November, a party of Spanish troops came upon them.

It was the time of truth. Had the news of Mexican independence been wrong? Were Becknell and his men to be arrested like McKnight? The friendly faces and hospitable gestures of Commander Pedro Gallego and his men quickly answered that question. This time the Mexicans had successfully revolted against Spain. There were now two large independent democracies inhabiting the North American continent. The men from the two republics camped together that night. The next day Becknell and his men rode into the village of San Miguel, not far from present-day Las Vegas, New Mexico. The local folk received them hospitably. Then it was on to Santa Fe.

Fifteen years before, the explorer Zebulon Pike had visited Santa Fe. Like most other Americans to enter the town, he was detained, but when he returned to the States, he described the high retail prices in Santa Fe, resulting from markups due to the long supply route from central Mexico. For instance, a Spanish yard (thirty-three inches) of common muslin cloth could cost New Mexicans as much as $3. In the western United States, it could be bought for about 10 cents. Missourians had dreamed of breaking into that market ever since. Becknell's company had only about $300 worth of trade goods. Would they be able to parlay that puny sum into a small fortune?

The answer was yes. Becknell's saddlebag quickly filled with silver. Ironically, these riches came when his fortunes were at low ebb. Back home in Missouri, he owed lots of money to creditors.

William Becknell was born in Virginia in 1787. He spent his early years in that state. Shortly after his wedding in 1807, he moved to Missouri. He labored in the saltworks at Booneslick. During the War of 1812, he worked his way through the ranks, starting as a sergeant and being promoted to ensign (second lieutenant) by war's end. After the war his prospects seemed bright. He operated a ferry across the Missouri and made a profit on every vehicle or passenger who headed west. Then his world grew darker. His wife died, and at the same time there was a financial panic. Money to pay off business loans taken in good times was hard to come by now. Turning to politics, Becknell ran for office in the first Missouri state legislature. He lost.

In the summer of 1821, rumors again circulated of a rebellion in Mexico. In a desperate gamble William placed an ad in the local paper, the *Missouri Intelligencer*. He called for men to set out on a supposed expedition to trade with the Comanche Indians, but left unsaid was the true nature of the venture. Each man had to supply himself with his own guns, a horse, and $10 to buy trade goods. The company profits would be divided equally. At least five joined him. It was illegal for Americans to cross west of the Missouri state line. Those lands were reserved for the exclusive use of the Indians. Only traders were allowed to go onto the plains. Becknell obtained the necessary permission by claiming the purpose of the expedition was to trade with the Comanche. His real purpose was to go to New Mexico.

On September 1 his company set out. They lay up for a few days at Fort Osage, near present-day Kansas City, and then began their epic journey. For the first few days, the country reminded Becknell and his men of Missouri. It was rolling and appeared green and very fertile. The only difference was the diminishing amount of timber, found only along the watercourses and in favorable locations. Though by now, mid-September, the heat was terrific. While chasing an elk he had wounded, Becknell was almost overcome by heatstroke. Or was it nerves? Many of his men also suffered from the heat or anxiety. After all Becknell had fibbed to his own government about his activities, and no one could say how the new Mexican government would greet them, or even if the Mexicans were actually free from Spain.

Determined "not to surrender to trifles," Becknell pushed his company across the plains. By the third week of September, they were in buffalo country. No timber was to be seen except a few scattered cottonwoods along the streams. But buffalo were everywhere at hand. When they arrived at the Arkansas River, they had traveled all day within sight of the large, shaggy creatures. They were now in a territory altogether different from any they had ever known. Even the animals were different. There were pronghorn antelope, which they called goats. The antelope were too fast for them to bring down with a bullet. The common rabbit of the area, now known as the black-tailed jackrabbit, had a dark tail and extremely large ears, quite a different sight from the cottontail rabbits the men were used to seeing. Finally, it was as big as a small dog and as fast as the antelope.

Becknell described another animal none of the company had any familiarity with: the badger. Its two-inch-long toenails amazed Becknell. So did its ability to use those nails to burrow after prairie dogs. Becknell said its meat was sweet to eat. Prairie dogs also really intrigued Becknell, as they have amused many since. He was amazed at the way the entire population of a prairie dog town would set up a chorus on the approach of danger. He liked the way they would sit in their holes, on mounds slightly above the plain, their forelegs exposed, until an intruder came too close, and then they'd duck into their burrows. Another strange animal to see running loose was the horse. Herds of them were encountered from time to time.

Becknell's company followed the Arkansas River west. They braved tall sand dunes and were forced to use dried buffalo dung for fuel. It served the purpose well enough, burning hot but fast. Although supposedly Indian traders, they remarked that they were pleased that they did not meet up with any "wild" Indians. Somewhere in what is now eastern Colorado, they found a lake. The residue left by the water reminded them of the saltpeter they used to make gunpowder. Truly this was an unusual country.

Becknell decided to forgo the easier pass at Raton going over the Rockies into New Mexico, instead taking the pass Stephen Long's expedition of the previous year had used. Later the Santa Fe Trail would cross at Raton. But Becknell and his men made it over the mountains. They found their way to Santa Fe and a windfall of trade. His saddlebags chinking with silver, Becknell determined to cross back over the plains to Missouri in midwinter. He had debts to pay off. As a further incentive, another party of Americans, the McKnight-James group, had blundered into Santa Fe a few days after Becknell's. Becknell may have determined to make that dangerous winter trek to be assured his men would reach home first and receive the credit due them.

In the days before weather forecasts, the plains were an extremely dangerous place. There was little shelter or fuel, and a blizzard could blow up in a twinkling. Many a traveler rued the day he decided to head across the plains in winter. But Becknell's luck would hold. Leaving most of his men to winter in Santa Fe, he departed on December 13 with eighteen inches of snow on the ground. The trek took about a month and a half, but he arrived safe and sound in Franklin, Missouri, in February. The coin he brought back was so plentiful he dumped his saddlebags on the sidewalk and watched silver bounce into the gutter—or so legend has it. A generous number of mules were included in his horse train. This started the trade in what would become a state icon, the so-called Missouri mule.

A few months later, on May 22, Becknell set off again for Santa Fe. His train included three wagons, thus marking the first time wheeled vehicles rolled across the prairie, since Oñate's wagons had crossed the plains in 1601. Just as importantly, knowing wagons could not be hied across the mountain pass in the Rockies, he blazed a shortcut from the Arkansas River to the Cimarron. The development of the Cimarron route along with the first use of wagons secured for Becknell the nickname of Father of the Santa Fe Trail. He did not long stay in the business of trading, leaving that to professional businessmen. He did, though, lead a party of trappers into the Colorado mountains in the mid-1820s. Later, he moved to Texas and took part in the Texas rebellion against Mexico. During World War II a Liberty ship was named for him.

GETTING THE BETTER OF THE
WHITE MAN AGAIN—AND AGAIN

- 1825 -

THE WHITE MAN NAMED GEORGE SIBLEY ROSE from the bench on which the three official Indian commissioners were seated. Pawhuska squatted in the sun on the other side of a camp table. The leaders of the Osage and the Little Osage Indians sat around him. Their brawny chests were bare. Their scalps were plucked smooth except for one lock of hair into which feathers were knotted. That is, all heads were bare except for Pawhuska, who wore a tattered periwig, the kind of wig worn during the colonial period. This periwig, along with the white man's nickname of White Hair, had been passed on to him by his father. On the table lay an official-looking document, several quill pens, and a pot of ink. The document was a treaty. The whites wanted to take something that belonged to the Osage. Pawhuska, the chief of the Big Osage, was sure the Americans wouldn't outwit him this time.

Pawhuska had allowed the whites to sit in the shade under the enormous oak tree, forever after known as Council Oak. He and the other Indians took their seats in the sun. It was August, and the heat was oppressive, a combination of the blast furnace ferocity of the desert off to the west and the cloying moistness of the woodlands to the east. The location where they were meeting was almost the exact dividing line between those climates, as shown by the last grove of hardwood trees growing on the prairie. It was okay with Pawhuska for the commissioners in their claw-tailed coats and enormous cravats to sit in the shade. He understood he had an advantage on them. He was just pretending the overdressed commissioners were the Indians' superiors and deserving of the shade. The more they sweltered in the heat the better the deal he might get for his people.

George Sibley slipped his hand into his hammer-tail coat. He raised his right hand. Pawhuska could tell the man was nervous. In spite of all, he was afraid the Osage wouldn't sign his document. Pawhuska had known Sibley for years. From 1808 until 1822, Sibley had served as Indian factor at Fort Osage near Independence, Missouri. The U.S. government designated the factor as the official trader to the Indians. Private trading was allowed, but the factor set fair prices for goods. As the third U.S. president, Thomas Jefferson had invented the so-called factory system. Jefferson felt dealing squarely with the Indians was a national obligation, but even before Jefferson died, the system was abolished. At that point George Sibley went into private Indian trade. As a good Presbyterian and a man who considered himself one of God's elect, Sibley just knew he would prosper in the private sector. After all one of the signs of the elect was material prosperity.

Of all people, George Sibley should have known better, because the people he was trading with were Pawhuska's Osage, an incredibly wily—and lucky—tribe. They had been getting the better of Sibley for years. At first it was government money he was losing, but once his dealings with them went private, they pushed him to the point of bankruptcy. However, at the moment Sibley carried on with all the dignity of a lawyer arguing a case before the Supreme Court. When he finished, leather-clad Bill Williams, an Osage trader, translated his remarks. Sibley pointed at the document on the table. He wanted the assembled company of Indians to come mark the document.

With a gleam in his eye, Pawhuska leapt to his feet and strode to the table. He dipped his thumb in the ink pot and boldly stamped the digit to paper. He winked at Sibley, who pretended not to notice. While the white man quickly scribbled the name *Pawhuska* next to the thumbprint, the Osage leader turned from the table. He motioned for Ca-he-wa-ga-ton-ega of the Little Osage to come forward. Some of the younger warriors glared at Pawhuska. An especially impertinent one grumbled that Pawhuska was a fool. He said, "You are giving away a ten-mile strip of land through the heart of our hunting grounds, Pawhuska." He railed against the white man's wagons traversing their lands to Santa Fe. He objected to them killing the Osage buffalo. All for a few dollars in cheap trade goods.

But Pawhuska just laughed. He believed the white man's wagons would go to Santa Fe whether the Osage permitted it or not. Besides, he knew the young man was angry for another reason. He thought he hadn't gotten as much of the trade goods as he believed were his due.

But the young warrior's words stayed the hand of the chief of the Little Osage.

Pawhuska had to urge him to sign. He pointed at the periwig on his head. He said it had been taken from a white man in what the whites called the Revolutionary War by his grandfather. Pawhuska was certain the Osage had been cleverer than the whites then, and he was equally certain they were outwitting the white man again with this treaty.

Ca-he-wa-ga-ton-ega was not quite as confident as Pawhuska. Sure, he liked his share of the $300 in goods—muskets, coats, beads, and liquor—that Sibley had distributed to him. And he was looking forward to claiming his share of the $500 in credit awarded them at Chouteau's trading post. But he was nagged by the fact that fewer than twenty years before, the Osage had controlled much of what today is Missouri, Arkansas, Kansas, and Oklahoma. Now they only had their holdings in Kansas and Oklahoma, which were now threatened as well.

Nothing to worry about, Pawhuska told him. Just thumb the document. Since there was really no alternative, because he had already accepted the goods, Ca-he-wa-ga-ton-ega shrugged and thumbed the document.

So who were these Osage who were confident in their ability to manipulate the various peoples that inhabited the midcontinent in the early nineteenth century? The short answer is that at the beginning of the Santa Fe trade, they controlled, more or less, half the territory the Santa Fe Trail traversed. Even more surprisingly, considering their fairly low modern profile, they were arguably the most powerful Indian tribe, bar none, in the region.

The Osage were a Dhegian-Siouan people, related remotely to the better-known Dakota Sioux of the upper Midwest and plains. They originally hailed from the forests east of the Mississippi. The massive dislocation caused by the coming of the whites in the seventeenth century drove the Osage out of the mid–Ohio River region and across the Father of Waters. They awed early travelers by their physical stature. Many early authorities claimed there was hardly an Osage male who was less than six feet. Washington Irving called the Osage, whom he had met on a hunting trip to the prairie, "the finest-looking Indians I have ever seen in the West." He also described them as "stately fellows; stern and simple in garb and aspect . . . Their heads were bare; their hair was cropped close, excepting a bristling ridge on the top, like the crest of a helmet, with a long scalp-lock hanging behind. They had fine Roman countenances, and broad deep chests; and, as they generally wore their blankets wrapped round their loins so as to leave the bust and arms bare, they looked like so many noble bronze figures."

The Osage occupied the country between the European settlements on the east and the prairie Indians to the West. They made a point of keeping up friendships with the whites. By doing so they controlled the trade of key goods such as firearms, gunpowder, and whiskey. The early Spanish explorers—Coronado in the 1540s and Oñate in 1602—found prosperous villages of Wichita Indians on the high plains. The Osage, armed and mounted, swooped down on these tribes. The Wichita were driven south to the Red River on the Oklahoma-Texas border. Having learned their lesson, the Wichita fortified their villages with log palisades. They forged alliances with the more warlike Comanche. All this allowed the Wichita to just barely hang on. The Pawnee were driven north to Nebraska. A frontier synonym for slave became pani (or Pawnee).

The Osage weren't the first to acquire the horse on the prairie. The so-called Plains Paducah, or Plains Apaches, related to the Lipan Apaches of Texas, got horses from the Spanish in New Mexico. They also adopted the Spanish lance and rawhide armor. The Paducah plundered neighboring villages. Suddenly, the Osage, armed with European firearms and the horse, set out to meet them. Even before Europeans arrived, the Osage had decimated the Plains Paducah. Remaining bands merged with the Kiowa and Jicarilla Apaches. After 1750 the Comanche sometimes came to be called the Paducah. At this point the Osage transferred their hostilities to those people. The Comanche, generally regarded as the fiercest raiders of the southern plains, complained about the Osage. "They steal our horses and murder our people," a Comanche chief commented. "The Americans sell them the arms and ammunition."

When the United States acquired the Louisiana Purchase, the Osage claimed most of Missouri south of the river, much of the northern half of Arkansas, most of Oklahoma excluding the panhandle, and an area in Kansas south of the Kansas and Smoky Hill Rivers out to the hundredth meridian. The Osage never warred openly with the American government, but they treated roughly individual trespassers, pretending to be friends when they often acted like enemies. In a list of violence perpetrated against whites drawn up by Jedediah Smith, the Osage were indicated as culprits many times more often than the supposedly hostile Comanche.

The Osage were vicious rivals. In 1833 a band of Osage warriors under Chief Clermont discovered an undefended Kiowa village near present-day Fort Sill, Oklahoma. They looted the camp, burned the teepees, and then scalped and decapitated the dead. Into each of the more than a hundred brass kettles discovered in the camp was put a head. A more powerful no-trespassing sign could hardly be imagined. This sort of activity, vicious as it was, kept the Santa Fe Trail relatively safe to the boundary of the Osage hunting grounds. During the Civil War the Osage proved themselves staunch Union allies. A detail of Southern sympathizers, led by a "so-called Colonel Harrison," set out to the West, probably intending to disrupt traffic along the Santa Fe and other trails. The Osage ran most of the sixteen to twenty-three men in the command to ground, with only two escaping. The heads of the dead were impaled on spikes.

Therefore, in 1825 Pawhuska signed the treaty at Council Grove with perfect confidence. Earlier that spring he had signed another treaty in Saint Louis. The first treaty gave up rights to the territory that the Santa Fe traversed. So why not sign another treaty and receive the treaty goods? The land might already have been lost, the way the whites saw things. But the country was uninhabited and would remain so for many years to come. Neither Pawhuska nor any other Osage had the least intention of ceasing to hunt buffalo on that land.

As the years wore on, the Osage were pushed—by more treaties—farther west into Kansas. By about the Civil War, they were pushed into Oklahoma. However, that did not mean that Pawhuska had made a mistake. In Oklahoma the Osage got the last laugh. The lands portioned out to them lay smack on top of a vast oil reserve. In 1906 the tribe had amassed $8,562,690 in the bank. The approximately three thousand Osage were considered the richest people on the planet. By 1925 their per capita income had soared to about $13,000, about $150,000 today. Rolls-Royces were as common as sparrows in Pawhuska, the county seat named for the periwig-wearing signer of the 1825 treaty.

THE CIMARRON DESERT
CLAIMS A HERO

- 1831 -

THIS WASN'T SUPPOSED TO HAPPEN—at least not to Jedediah Smith and Thomas "White Hair" Fitzpatrick. They were two of the West's savviest explorers and mountain men. Each had endured innumerable Indian attacks. They had crossed countless deserts without roads or trails to guide them. They couldn't be on the point of foundering. Not here in what was to become the southwestern part of the state of Kansas. But as they stared at the dry hole that was called Lower Spring, they knew they were in dire peril. And so were the seventy-four men in their wagon train, who were depending on the two adventurers' finding water.

Fitzpatrick dropped to his knees. With his one good hand, he scooped sand. Not so much as bead of sweat bound the grains in his palm. Impatiently, Smith pushed Fitzgerald out of the way. With the butt of his musket, he shoveled frantically. He tore at the slight depression like a badger after a prairie dog. Then his energy gave out. It was no use. The hole was dry.

Fitzgerald was too used up to move on. Smith ordered him to continue excavations in hopes of digging down to the water table. He said he'd drop down into the bed of the Cimarron River and then check out the broken ground three miles yonder. He'd encountered a spring in that area in an earlier pass through the region.

Smith held out little hope for the sandy channel of the Cimarron. The stream was sometimes called the Dry Cimarron. It rarely ran and most of the time didn't even contain pools of water. And when there were pools, they were usually too bitter and alkaline to drink. Nonetheless, he gave a start when he found the winding channel bone dry. He spurred his horse. There was no time to spare.

Jedediah owned eleven of the twenty-odd wagons in the caravan strung out behind. The other ten belonged to David Jackson and William Sublette. The three men had owned a fur-trading company in the mountains of the Northwest. They had decided to move to the Southwest because of the cutthroat competition from other trading companies and, worst of all, the danger posed by the Blackfeet Indians. The men were confident in their abilities. Jackson, after whom Jackson Hole in present-day Wyoming is named, was a veteran of the Battle of New Orleans. White Hair Fitzpatrick, to whom the former partners sold their fur company, got his nickname from his head turning gray in a period of days while hiding out from those dreadful Blackfeet. But all these men took their hats off to Jedediah Smith when it came to mastery of wilderness ways.

Once "Old Jed" (he was twenty-four at the time) had been mauled by a grizzly bear. He instructed a member of his party to sew his ear and scalp back on. He took off two weeks to recuperate. Then he resumed his duties as captain of that party. For all his toughness Jedediah Smith did not use tobacco or alcohol. He was celibate, pious, Bible reading, serious, and responsible to a fault. These things could be said of practically no other mountain man.

On the journey that involved the bear attack, Jedediah had saved two dehydrating companions by covering them in cool sand and forging ahead for water. In the years since, he had covered many miles in the West. His job was to explore for new beaver-trapping country. Jed was the first to follow the Green River in southwestern Wyoming, over mountains and through deserts, to its junction with the Colorado River. He followed the channel to the Mojave Desert. He then crossed to the Mexican missions at what would become Los Angeles, California. From there he made his way north to San Francisco Bay. Leaving most of the company to winter in California, he and his two companions transited the Sierra Nevada, the first Americans to do so.

They then traversed the Great Basin Desert of Nevada and Utah. His two companions dropped for lack of water, but Jedediah plodded on and discovered some small springs near the Great Salt Lake. He safely retrieved his men. Later that year, 1827, he retraced his path to California. On that occasion Havasupai Indians attacked him as he was ferrying supplies to the California side of the Colorado River. He lost most of his trade goods but continued on to northern California. Acquiring three hundred head of horses, he drove the animals to Oregon by swimming them in the ocean surf because the coast mountains were too high and thickly wooded to go over. His party was set upon on the Umpqua River by Kelawatset Indians. Jedediah and two others escaped the ambush. They made their way back to the annual rendezvous of mountain men in the northern Rockies.

Jedediah traveled through very wild and unsettled country. He moved on horseback, by canoe, and on foot, much of the time in very dangerous circumstances.

After all of that, there was little about the Santa Fe Trail or the Cimarron Desert that gave Jed and his companions pause. Still, taking nothing for granted, they had outfitted their caravan with a six-pound cannon.

But the artillery piece had proved of little help less than a week before at Pawnee Rock. There one of the hands, E. S. Minter, had set out to hunt antelope. He was killed and scalped by Pawnees.

A couple of days later, Jedediah Smith reined his mule into the shade of a cottonwood on the bank of the Arkansas River, near present-day Dodge City, Kansas. Jedediah gazed across the stream. The dunes on the far bank were Mexican territory. He didn't like what he was seeing. He didn't mind heading into a foreign country. Nor did the sand hills bother him. But sand dunes were never a good thing when you had a caravan of twenty-two heavily loaded wagons. And dunes were even worse news in an extraordinarily dry spell when the sand crumbled and the narrow wheels sank as though in quicksand.

Across the Arkansas River lay the most dreaded stretch of the Santa Fe Trail, the so-called Cimarron Desert. No water was to be had for fifty or sixty miles—no one knew exactly how far. And not even that was what most concerned him. All old trail hands knew the story of one of the first wagon trains that attempted to cross that desert. It had happened nine years before. The terrain stretched perfectly flat, with few trees or ravines to mark the way, and the caravan had become horribly lost. All about, lakes of water beckoned—tantalizing but deadly mirages. When those early teamsters had almost reached the banks of the Cimarron, most of them, mad from thirst, foolishly turned around and dashed headlong back to the Arkansas, meaning almost certain death. By dumb luck, one of those who persevered spotted a lone buffalo bull, its gut dragging. Backtracking the animal's trail led to the river—and, for once, water. That wagon train was saved.

But none of that bothered Jedediah as much as the little black dots he was seeing everywhere on the other side of the river.

The best part of a week later, Jed came to understand what it was about those little black dots that concerned him. The dots had been buffalo, more than he had ever seen before. Their deep, worn trails crisscrossed the sandy plain of the Cimarron Desert, obscuring the trail of previous wagon trains. In a repeat of that early caravan's ordeal, the traders wandered, lost, for three days. Each day the water in the five-gallon keg carried in each wagon diminished. The dray mules were braying from thirst, on the point of foundering. Someone had to discover water.

Clearly the man for the job was Jed Smith.

Jed had learned that in areas of internal drainage, springs could be found below outcroppings. Taking Fitzpatrick with him, he found what trail hands called Lower Spring. He left Fitzpatrick to dig down in the sand, and Jedediah made for Fargo Spring, which he had stumbled across in an earlier crossing of the plains. His nose for water told him that spot was his best hope.

In this instance Jedediah was wrong. Fargo too was dry. While Jedidiah was on hands and knees desperately scooping sand, a dozen Comanche swooped down on him. The Indians spread out like an encircling net. Jedediah tried to keep the warriors from getting behind him. A Comanche fired. The bullet smashed Jed's left shoulder blade. Though terribly wounded, Jedediah turned his rifle on the Comanche leader. The single explosion killed the warrior. Before Jed could draw his pistols, the Indians were on him. They thrust their lances, stabbing him.

Thus ended the career of the early West's greatest explorer. Ironically, Jedediah and his partners believed the Santa Fe trade was less dangerous than continuing along what is now the Canadian border. The Blackfeet Indians were much to be feared. But as Jedediah found out, so were the Comanche.

OLD BILL WILLIAMS MAKES
THE TRADE OF HIS LIFE

- 1836 -

In the far distance William S. Williams spied the castlelike fort on banks of the Arkansas River. Digging his spurs into the flanks of his mare, he snatched his hat and screeched, "He-haw." The horses and mules in the cavvyard, or herd, in front of him danced excitedly. His two companions, seeing his movement, goaded their mounts forward, stirring up the three hundred anxious animals. A choking cloud of dust rose from the hooves of the prancing animals. The men and horses were swallowed by it. A glint of satisfaction in his eye, Old Bill Williams tore hell-bent for the fort. He was in the middle of a stampede. And he was loving it.

He and his two companions had rounded up this herd of free-ranging horses in California. Then they had driven the animals across the Mojave Desert and the arid wastes of what would become Nevada, Utah, and western Colorado. After all of that, Old Bill wasn't going to be deprived of one final prank—scaring the daylights out of the inhabitants of the fort looming ahead of him. He saw the twinkle of a glass catching the sun in the tower, where a powerful brass telescope was kept. The proprietor was trying to determine if the dust cloud the horses were stirring up was an army of marauders.

The fort was not that different from a medieval European castle. It sported battlements and turrets. Its thick, high, cactus-guarded walls stretched in a trapezoid 137 feet by 178 feet. Like many medieval castles it was situated in a strategic spot on a river. Its guns were placed to defend the walls, tearing to pieces any body of men trying to storm them. But the edifice was constructed of dried mud bricks ten inches wide by two inches high by eighteen inches long. The Stars and Stripes flew from the tall mast in the courtyard. Situated on the plains of eastern Colorado, it wasn't far from where the Santa Fe Trail crossed the Arkansas and beelined to Raton Pass for its descent to New Mexico.

After running the herd around the fort, Old Bill drew up to the gate on the east side of the structure. The proprietor of the fort, William Bent, was a small man. The youngest of three partners, he along with his brother, Charles Bent, and Ceran St. Vrain built it. Bent slouched in the entryway. He made a determined effort not to show the fright Old Bill knew he had given him.

"Wagh, old hoss," Bill addressed him.

"How, Bill!" Mr. Bent asked. "How'd you come by these horses?"

"Is that any business of yours?"

"I was just asking out of curiosity."

"Truth to tell, Bent, they come from Californy. A posse of Californians set out after these here horses, which they thought was their own. Me and the boys had to separate the deputation's horses from themselves, leaving them afoot."

Mr. Bent just nodded.

"Bent," Old Bill went on. "Take all these horses and roll out that barrel of whiskey that's been in the storeroom so long. I'll kill it or it shall kill me."

Bent shrugged his agreement. The barrel of whiskey was rolled out, and a colossal party was had by one and all.

Born in North Carolina in 1787, Bill Williams was brought by his parents to the Spanish territory of Missouri when he was five years old. Bill learned to read and write from his mother. Because of his rather unusual ability to read the Bible, he set himself up—while still in his teens—as circuit-riding parson. Legend has it he gave up preaching to his white flock when a young woman in the congregation spurned Bill's offer of marriage. Abandoning the company of white people entirely, he took his ministry to the Osage Indians. Raised on the frontier, Bill early on had learned to speak Osage. More importantly, he represented a valuable resource to the tribe. He could explain, interpret, and intercede with the whites for them.

Bill may have started out as a minister, but as time wore on, he crossed one line after another. Given his high spirits, it was probably inevitable that he ride with young Osage men on raids for ponies and scalps. Finally, his religious convictions went, and he came to adopt Indian beliefs. He, along with Kit Carson and many other mountain men, believed in signs and omens. For instance, Old Bill held bears in dread. He had a vision that foretold his death should a bear place a paw on his shoulder. Shortly before he was killed, he had a dream in which a bear laid its paws on his shoulders. Oddly enough, he dismissed this nocturnal omen.

For almost twenty years Bill lived among the Osage. Sometimes he was paid to be the official interpreter at Fort Osage. At times he traded among the Osage nation. He failed as an Osage trader because his Osage in-laws demanded credit that seldom was repaid. At other times he trapped and traded with other tribes. In 1822 he made more than a thousand dollars in this trade, a fortune then.

His great contribution to the Santa Fe Trail occurred on August 9, 1825, when he was thirty-eight years old. He translated the treaty talks with the Osage that gave the Americans right of passage of the Santa Fe Trail. This council changed most profoundly the life of Bill Williams. Afterward, he accepted a job to continue on with the expedition. He was paid $33.33 a month and a horse. After he completed these duties, Bill kept on going down the trail. And he never looked back. His career as a plainsman was finished. From now on he was Old Bill Williams, mountain man. He acquired the "old" part of his name because he was almost a generation older than his peers. As his biographer Alpheus Favour says, "What he as a young man, would have revolted against, now seemed second nature; and what he, as a young man, had valued, had entirely lost its attractiveness. Houses, dress, books, cleanliness, restraint, and the refinements of civilization had become irksome and of no interest to him."

The territory Old Bill covered in the next twenty-three years would impress a cross-country trucker. He rented several traps and headed alone into the mountains of New Mexico and Colorado. The next spring he sold $1,100 worth of pelts at Bent's Fort. He took to signing himself "Bill Williams, Master Trapper." A Ute Indian said he was "a great trapper, a great hunter, took many beaver, and a great warrior—his belt was full of many scalps; but no friend, no squaw, he was always by himself."

The following years found Bill on the Columbia River, in the Yellowstone country, on the upper Missouri, and around the Great Salt Lake. In all these areas Bill was a legend even among mountain men. They admired his famous "double wobble" with which he sighted his gun. Even though he was known as a dead shot, he never bothered holding his rifle steady. His gun always "wobbled." He was also known for his shambling, lopsided gait. He staggered along on one side and then the other. Long after he came to be called "Old

Bill," he claimed to be able to outrun any man, even with thirty pounds of beaver traps on his own back.

He was just as famous for his bets and his pranks. He claimed to have lost $1,000 to a fellow mountain man on a single hand of the card game seven-up. He once "attacked" a detail of soldiers, riding toward them in a frightening manner, and then ran away until they gave chase. When finally run down, he had a good laugh even though he was slapped in irons and hauled back across the plains to Fort Leavenworth.

He returned to Bent's Fort on the mountain route of the Santa Fe Trail in the late fall of 1847 when Major John C. Fremont was outfitting an expedition to cross the Rocky Mountains in the dead of winter. The most controversial chapter in Old Bill William's life was about to begin. Major Fremont had been officially rebuked for, without orders, capturing California and setting himself up as governor at the outset of the Mexican-American War. Fremont marched an expedition down the Santa Fe Trail to Bent's Fort to recoup his reputation. He planned to forge directly west into the Colorado Rockies, instead of veering south into New Mexico. Experienced local mountain men at Bent's Fort, such as "Uncle Dick" Wootton, said a winter crossing could not be accomplished. But Old Bill agreed to act as guide.

Fremont has to be given high marks for fortitude and confidence. The thermometer dropped below zero. Snow piled up to more than twenty feet. Fremont plugged on. He conquered the Sangre de Cristo Range but ran afoul of the San Juans on the far side of the Rio Grande. Food for the animals ran out, and then went the food for the men.

Finally, even Fremont realized the jig was up. He cached the expedition's gear and sent a relief party of four, including Old Bill, ahead. The relief party grew so weak one of their members died. Fremont, coming up from behind, passed them. In later years he claimed Old Bill had feasted on the dead man. Altogether ten members of the expedition perished, and Old Bill became Fremont's scapegoat. The military officer claimed he was misled at every turn by the mountain man. Of Old Bill, Kit Carson supposedly said, "In starving times no man who ever knew him walked in front of Bill Williams."

Bill died before he had a chance to defend himself. His friends claimed he was loyally trying to retrieve Fremont's gear. His detractors said his death came about because of a dispute dividing the plunder. One member of Fremont's expedition took Old Bill's side. He named Old Bill Williams Mountain just north of Prescott, Arizona, for Bill. The town of Williams, Arizona, commemorates his name as does a nearby river. Most impressively, however, is a modern organization in Arizona called the Old Bill Williams Mountain Men. That organization, which until recently was honorarily chaired by a U.S. senator, keeps Old Bill's memory alive.

A NOBLE DIES
ON THE SANTA FE TRAIL

- 1843 -

STANDING ON THE EDGE OF THE DIRT BANK, Don Antonio Chavez knew he had only one chance to live. He had to tell this man who called himself a captain what he wanted to know. And what he wanted to know was the hiding place of Don Antonio's money.

So tell him, Don Antonio counseled himself. *Your money will do you no good if you are dead.* But Don Antonio didn't tell him. He couldn't tell him. The man was his enemy. It wasn't simply that he was his enemy because he was a thief. He was a thief, all right. But he was his enemy because he was an enemy of his country—of both of Don Antonio's countries, Mexico and New Mexico.

The story of Don Antonio Chavez started far away two years previously in Texas. Texas, at the time, considered itself an independent country. Texas rebels, who included American and Mexican nationals, had fought the Mexican government in a series of battles. They had lost all of them, except for the last one, the Battle of San Jacinto.

At that battle the Mexican forces were routed and their commander, General Santa Anna, was captured. After Santa Anna agreed to recognize Texas independence, he was released and sent back to Mexico. Sam Houston, the leader of the Texas army, was elected president of the republic. He was defeated for a second term by a man of an entirely different disposition, Mirabeau B. Lamar. Lamar hatched the so-called Texan–Santa Fe Expedition.

Texas claimed all of the territory on its side of the Rio Grande, from its source in the Rocky Mountains to its mouth in the Gulf of Mexico. This meant that all of New Mexico west of the Rio Grande was also claimed by Texas. In order to establish Texas's claim to this land and divert the Santa Fe trade to Texas, Lamar proposed an expedition to New Mexico. The caravan was made up of twenty-some wagons loaded with goods for trade. But more tellingly, it was escorted and protected by a military guard of 320 men. To the New Mexicans, those 320 men appeared to be a conquering force, and probably that's what Lamar had in mind. The military commander even had a company of artillery, hardly necessary for purely defensive purposes. The expedition set out from near Austin in June of 1841.

The one thing Lamar didn't count on was the terrain. It was a desert, so finding enough water for the huge command was always a problem. Furthermore, the territory was completely unknown. No one knew where he was going exactly, just west and a bit north. And then things got worse. Indians attacked their force, and they ran out of food. But, finally, the Texans made contact with New Mexicans in September. The governor of New Mexico was Manuel Armijo, one of the more interesting figures in the history of the Santa Fe Trail. In many ways he resembled the Texas president Lamar. He was shrewd and, by many accounts, not altogether honest. It turned out he was more than a match for Lamar and his Texan–Santa Fe Expedition.

The Texans arrived in New Mexico destitute. They were out of food and needed water. Their army was broken and not fit to fight. Armijo, through intermediaries, promised them aid if they laid their weapons aside. They did, and they were fed. Then they were arrested, clapped in irons, and marched south to Old Mexico to prison. Texans, forgetting about their attempt to conquer the territory, were outraged. They felt their countrymen had been treated unfairly.

Remember, to Texans all of the territory on their side of the Rio Grande was Texas. This meant all of the Santa Fe Trail from present-day Dodge City all the way to Santa Fe belonged to Texas. Anyone traveling that route, according to the Texans, was trespassing. To even the score, the Texans commissioned a group of rangers to patrol the Santa Fe Trail. Any caravan of New Mexicans would be captured and plundered. Although supposedly commissioned by a government entity, these rangers were widely regarded as "land pirates."

One of the worst of those officially appointed was a criminal by the name of John McDaniel. He had spent some time in Texas. Evidently he had to leave because of his work as a robber. None of this was evidently known or mattered to the Texas agent who found him in Missouri. He was given the rank of captain and allowed to raise a company of compatriots. His mission was to raid Mexican caravans on that portion of the Santa Fe Trail claimed by Texas.

In the meantime, in New Mexico things were in terrible confusion. By the early 1840s most of the local Santa Fe trade was in the hands of New Mexicans themselves. After all they understood the local people's needs and wants better than any foreign merchants could. And now there were rumors of Texas raiders and also attempts by the Mexican government to completely forbid trade with the United States. To avoid both of these possibilities, young Antonio Chavez, the son of the first governor of New Mexico after independence, decided to get an early start. He took only two wagons, but his complement of twenty men and fifty-five mules was strong enough to see him through, he believed. He is said to have carried in the wagons several bales of furs and $12,000 in silver money. The small caravan departed in February.

Crossing the prairie in the winter was always a dicey proposition. One of the things a traveler did not want to see was remarkably fine weather. That almost always foretold a looming cold front and blizzard. Sure enough, on the deadly Cimarron River, the snowstorm struck. All fifty-five mules froze to death. Chavez was set afoot on the barren plains. Then worse fortune struck. Fifteen of his men deserted. Chavez cached the furs in underground pits. Weighed down by the silver coin, the small expedition struggled along by shank's mare.

By April 10 the small band arrived at the Little Arkansas River, in present east central Kansas. There they met Captain John McDaniel and his fifteen raiders. The locale was well within U.S. territory, but McDaniel immediately stripped Chavez's party of its valuables. Only $2,000 was found. Chavez had squirreled away the funds. McDaniel learned of the presence of the further funds from men in the party.

Bad luck plagued all involved in this venture, victims and land pirates alike. Some of McDaniel's men wanted to split the plunder and move on. Others were for torturing Chavez and company until all the silver was disgorged. By a freak coincidence, while the Texas agents were trying to figure the best thing to do, all their horses strayed—or were stolen by Indians. That was a sign for seven of McDaniel's men. They took their share of the plunder and hoofed it back to Missouri.

McDaniel tried to induce Don Antonio to divulge the location of his money. No amount of torture worked. Finally, McDaniel put his revolver to Don Antonio's head, demanding, "Tell me or you die." Don Antonio had already sized McDaniel up for the crook he was and come to the conclusion he would die in any case. He refused to talk. McDaniel shot him, and then he and his party took off on foot to Missouri.

Unfortunately for McDaniel, the Texas plot to disrupt trail traffic had been found out by the U.S. government. Troops had been dispatched to capture McDaniel. They missed him on the trail, but he was caught in Missouri. He was put on trial in Saint Louis. Don Antonio's sister or sister-in-law, depending on the version one reads, who had traveled across the plains with him, identified McDaniel. She told of his fiendish deeds. He and one other man were convicted and sentenced to hang. The others were sent to prison. The soldiers on the trail may have missed McDaniel but they found other Texas land pirates. They were arrested and also carried back to Missouri for trial.

In August of 1843, President Santa Anna of Mexico sealed the northern border after hearing of Don Antonio's death. He only reopened it in the spring of 1844 on news of McDaniel's execution. As a result of this tragedy and the subsequent justice it entailed, however, merchant traffic on the Santa Fe Trail was safer for peoples of all nationalities.

FRANCIS PARKMAN VISITS WESTPORT

- 1846 -

IN THE NINETEENTH CENTURY MANY SICKLY YOUNG MEN traveled West thinking the purity of the climate and the ruggedness of the trip would help make them strong. Francis Parkman, a recent graduate of Harvard College, was one of those. His jumping-off place for his great western journey was Kansas Landing, now part of Kansas City, Missouri. The Kansas City area was the staging ground for caravans that traveled the Santa Fe Trail, along with many of the wagon trains heading west on the Oregon Trail.

Parkman first oversaw the off-loading of his considerable frontier baggage, which included tents, guns, telescopes, saddles, harness, and so on. He also made sure that the French-style cart he bought in Saint Louis, called a mule-killer, got safely off the steamboat, the *Radnor*. It had taken the *Radnor* slightly more than a week to travel up the flood-swollen Missouri River from Saint Louis to Kansas Landing. In her cabins were "Santa Fe traders, gamblers, speculators and adventurers" and in the open steerage "were crowded Oregon emigrants, 'mountain men,' Negroes, and a party of Kansas Indians." Parkman watched the huge freight wagons made for the Santa Fe trade roll off the *Radnor* as he waited for his "mule-killer" cart. At the same time the party of Kansas Indians dressed themselves in the store-bought goods they procured in Saint Louis. Parkman remarked that they made a "striking and picturesque feature in the forest landscape" as they rode off.

Parkman and his cousin, Quincy A. Shaw, made their way five miles south to Westport. The town was becoming the leading land "port" of the traders. During the preceding decade Independence, nine miles east of Kansas Landing, had been the primary point of departure for Santa Fe traders. The evening before, when the *Radnor* had docked at Independence landing, Parkman had seen a party of thirty or forty Mexicans, hands for a Santa Fe trader, cooking around a campfire. Among them were a group of Indians from "a remote Mexican tribe." He also noted a couple of French trappers garbed in buckskin and three American mountain men with rifles across their knees.

Parkman and his cousin found Westport "was full of Indians, their shaggy little ponies were tied by dozens along the houses and fences. Sacs and Foxes, with shaved heads and painted faces, Shawnees and Delawares, fluttering in calico frocks and turbans. Wyandots dressed like white men, and a few Kansas wrapped in old blankets, were strolling about the streets or lounging in and out of the shops or houses."

The town was teeming with energy. One easterner said the following about a frontier community: "Besides these [Indians and white traders], there was a sprinkling of trappers, hunters, half-breeds, Creoles, Negroes, and all other beings that keep about the frontiers, between civilized and savage life. And withal the scene was one of complete bustle, the blacksmith shed, in particular was a scene of preparation, a strapping Negro was shoeing a horse, two half-breeds were fabricating iron spoons in which to melt lead for bullets. An old trapper, in leathern hunting-frock and moccasins, had placed his rifle against a work bench [from] which he superintended the operation and gossiped about his hunting exploits. Several large dogs were lounging in and out of the shop or sleeping in the sunshine. A little cur with head cocked on one side and one ear erect was watching, with that curiosity common to little dogs, the process of shoeing, as if studying the art or waiting for his turn to be shod."

Since Parkman was going to the mountains, he had to prepare himself like a mountain man. The most important equipment a mountain man carried was his rifle. He used it to feed and defend himself. And a man in Parkman's position wanted the best firearm he could find, which was probably a Hawken's he had bought in Saint Louis. If something was really good, early westerners would say, "It is a regular Hawken's," referring to a rifle made by gunsmiths Jake and Samuel Hawken. This very heavy rifle shot bullets that weighed about half an ounce. The wood stock ran up to the muzzle, a ferocious bull buffalo engraved on its butt. This rifle could be depended on to knock down and kill anything encountered on the plains or in the mountains—with deadly accuracy. Parkman's rifle weighed fifteen pounds

On a little stream beyond the town, the youths probably saw something like this scene reported by Frederick Ruxton:

> *Upwards of forty huge waggons [sic], of Conestoga*
> *and Pittsburgh build, and covered with snow-white*
> *tilts, were ranged in a semi-circle on the flat open*
> *prairie, their long tongues pointing outwards, with*
> *the necessary harness for four pairs of mules, or eight*

yoke of oxen, lying on the ground beside them, spread in ready order for "hitching up." Round the waggons [sic] groups of teamsters, tall stalwart young Missourians, were engaged in busy preparation for the start, greasing the wheels, fitting or repairing harness, smoothing oxbows or overhauling their moderate kits or "possibles" [the early western term for personal property]. They were all dressed in the same fashion, a pair of "homespun" pantaloons, tucked into thick boots reaching nearly to the knee, and confined around the waist by a broad leathern belt, which supported a strong butcher knife in a sheath. [The length of this knife, universally carried by Americans, caused them to be dubbed "long knives" by North American Indians.] A coarse checked shirt was their only covering, with a fur cap on the head.

Numerous campfires surrounded the waggons [sic], and by them lounged wild-looking mountaineers, easily distinguished from the "greenhorn" teamsters by their dresses of buckskin, and their weather-beaten faces. Without an exception, these were under the influence of the rosy god; and one, who sat, the picture of misery, at a fire by himself—staring into the blaze with vacant countenance, his long matted hair hanging in unkempt masses over his face, begrimed with the dirt of a week, and pallid with the effects of ardent drink—was suffering from the usual consequences of having "kept it up" beyond the usual point, and now was paying the penalty in a fit of "horrors."

In another part, the merchants of the caravan and Indian traders were superintending the lading of the waggons [sic], or mule packs. These were dressed in civilised attire, and some bedizened in St. Louis or Eastern City dandyism, to the infinite disgust of the mountain men, who look upon a bourge-way [bourgeois or boss] with most undisguised contempt. The picturesque appearance of the encampment was not a little heightened by the addition of several Indians from the neighboring Shawnee settlement, who, mounted on their small active horses on which they reclined, rather than sat, in negligent attitudes, quietly looked on at the novel scene, indifferent to the "chaff" which the thoughtless teamsters indulged in at their expense. Numbers of mules and horses were picketed at hand, while a large herd of noble oxen were being driven towards the camp—the wo-ha of the teamsters sounding far and near, as they collected the scattered beasts in order to yoke up.

Back in Westport proper, Parkman and Shaw noticed men packing bales and boxes into the huge freight wagons. When the mules were driven in from pasture, then teamsters had the tough job of catching the unruly animals, haltering them, and putting them in harnesses. After all that, the expedition got slowly into motion.

Another observer of similar scenes observed:

Every window sash is raised, and anxious faces appear watching with interest the departure. The drivers snap their long whips and swear at their unruly mules, bidding goodby between the oaths, to old friends on each side of the street as they move along. Accidents are very apt to occur on the occasion of a setting out. Sometimes the unmanageable mules will not stir at all, and then they are just as likely to take the opposite notion and run off with the enormous weight of merchandise behind them.

A drunken driver lashed his mules into a fright and then tumbled into the road, while the team dashed aside and dragged the loaded vehicle down a steep lane over stumps and stones and other inequalities with most dangerous velocity, until they were brought up against a log house in the middle of the way. Another accident happened before the wagons got well out of town. The fact was the drivers had all made the most of their last day in 'town.' In short most were dead drunk.

The young men also had a little trouble with their new cart. The shaft mule, like the freighters' mules, turned out to be completely uncontrollable. It reared and plunged and burst its harness. Parkman made his way to the middle of Westport and a redbrick store, owned by A. G. (Albert Gallatin) Boone, a grandson of the famous frontiersman. During this period he outfitted the Santa Fe trade. Later he would migrate west along the Santa Fe Trail and became a prominent figure, even starting another Booneville in Colorado. He shared the pleasant personality of his grandfather Daniel, cheerfully supplying the young men with a replacement animal. But the young men's troubles were not at an end. When Parkman and Shaw had hardly crossed into Kansas, the cart bounced into a deep, muddy gully. For an hour the men worked at extracting their conveyance. Sweaty and soiled, after coaxing the cart from the mud, they finally began their long, difficult, but fun-filled adventure on the prairie.

Their journey took them a few miles along the Santa Fe Trail, and then they marched north on the Oregon Trail. They spent the summer among the Sioux on the western plains. Returning, the young men dropped down along the face of the Rockies to Bent's Fort on the Arkansas River. They traveled to Westport on the Santa Fe Trail. Parkman spent the rest of his career as a professor at Harvard University and wrote many books dealing with frontier history. His experience on the Oregon and Santa Fe Trails went a long way to adding to his knowledge of the West.

A SOUTHERN LADY IN NEW MEXICO

- 1846 -

SUSAN SHELBY MAGOFFIN'S HUSBAND, JOSEPH MAGOFFIN, was a
Santa Fe trader. Like most traders that stayed in business for any
length of time, he was a shrewd businessman. And Susan had a new
opportunity for him selling tickets to see the latest local attraction—
Susan herself!

Susan's carriage had just driven down a hill and over a beautiful
little clear-running stream and into the village of Las Vegas, New
Mexico. Having stopped in a village, the travelers had no necessity to
stop and "noon it," that is, build a fire and make coffee and cook a
lunch. The driver went to find something to eat. Immediately the
children of Las Vegas crowded around the carriage. When Susan first
looked out of the carriage window, she saw a dozen kids. On her second look two dozen more appeared. They were of all ages, from those
just barely able to get around on their own to elementary school age.
None of them was fully dressed, and some of the little ones were
almost totally without clothes.

Susan, being a proper Southern lady, wore a hat with a veil. She drew the veil down over her face. She wanted to get a good look at the crowd around the carriage, without letting on what she was doing. In the meantime one of the men in the wagon train came to her. While she pretended to carry on a conversation with him, she eyed the kids. They were packed "so thick 'twas hard for anyone to pass; eyes were opened to their fullest extent, mouths gaped, tongues clattered, and I could only bite my lips and almost swallow my tongue to restrain my laughter."

What was so funny? Susan herself. She was the first American woman any of these children had ever seen, and one of the very first American women to ever go down the Santa Fe Trail. Even American men were not all that common in Las Vegas. But they passed through every now and then on Santa Fe–bound wagon trains. But most of them were from the rural backwoods farms and rather uncouth. Susan was different, a lot different. She not only was a woman; she was also a lady. Even the children seemed to understand she was a species all her own.

For her part Susan thought she was producing a regular "monkey show." She thought her husband, the shrewd trader he was, should allow the children to peep in for 2 or 3 reals each, that is 10 or 15 cents. Susan, of course, was only kidding, but her kidding shows the kind of person she was. She had agreed to set out, at the age of eighteen, as the only woman in a wagon train with twenty men. Those men were far from the genteel sort she knew back home in Kentucky. (Susan occasionally asked in her diary if it wouldn't be possible to drive a mule train with much less swearing.) For her honeymoon she and her husband had spent six months in New York and Philadelphia. Susan traveled with a driver, a maid, Jane, and three servant boys. Her "tent house" was custom made in Philadelphia, and it had a table that fastened to the tent pole. She had a traveling dressing bureau that held her combs, mirror, and so forth. Her camp bed was as good "as many houses have" with sheets, blankets, pillows, and a bedspread. The floor of her tent was carpeted, and she had folding camp stools to sit on. Even her maid had her own carriage.

But now the tables were turned on Susan. She was invited inside her first Mexican house for a Mexican meal. When she got inside the adobe house, not only the children but the adult women and men swarmed around her "like bees." This was a time when American women covered themselves in restrictive dresses from the neck right down to and including the feet. Perhaps Susan was fashionable but her style of clothing could hardly have been comfortable in the hot, dusty Southwest. The Mexican women were dressed only in blouses and skirts. Their feet were shod mostly in Indian moccasins, and over their shoulders were draped the "far-famed rebozos," long, colorful mantillas, or scarves, that all Mexican women wore all the time. Babies were wrapped up in some of the rebozos, and many of them were nursing. Susan, raised in a Victorian environment, found this dress style and the nursing babies shocking. Even more shocking to Susan was the fact that both genders smoked "little *cigarettas.*" These cigarettes were hand-rolled using homegrown tobacco and corn-husk wrappers. In Susan's day in the America east of the Mississippi, a lady never smoked.

But the strangest sight for Susan was the food. Set before her on a napkin were six thin pancakes, called by the strange name *tortillas.* A weird mixture of green peppers, onions, and meat, which Susan was told was called *chili con carne* was also set down in a clay pot along with some cheese. There was no fork, spoon, or knife. Susan was absolutely flabbergasted to learn she was supposed to roll the mixture in the tortilla. Roasted corn and a bowl of soup completed Susan's first meal in Mexico.

The village in which Susan was eating was barely inside the

strange new world of Hispanic America. Already New Mexico, though still completely Mexican in culture, had been annexed to the United States, thanks to the shrewd negotiations of her brother-in-law James Magoffin. She was to stay a little over a year and see many more strange and wonderful things. She would travel down the Camino Real Trail to El Paso and then beyond to the city of Chihuahua, Mexico. In front of her were the American forces fighting the Mexican-American War. Her husband sold the fourteen wagonloads of goods he imported into Mexico, and they made their way, following American troops, to Saltillo and Monterrey. They caught passage on a steamboat from Matamoros to New Orleans.

Susan, like many other frontierswomen, paid dearly for her adventure. While crossing Ash Creek in central Kansas, her carriage had overturned. She learned a few weeks later she was pregnant when she suffered a miscarriage at Bent's Old Fort. Then in Old Mexico she contracted yellow fever, and her second child was stillborn. Susan lived only a few more years, dying in 1855, barely nine years after the beginning of her great trek to the Southwest and Mexico. Her ill health was probably a result of the rigors she endured during her great adventure. Her husband retired to Saint Louis. After Susan's death Joseph Magoffin married her cousin, also named Susan, and lived until 1888.

LEWIS GARRARD AND FORT MANN

- 1847 -

AT SEVENTEEN YEARS OF AGE, LEWIS GARRARD, who grew up and went to school in Cincinnati, Ohio, thought he had just come to the end of the adventure of a lifetime. He was to learn that he could not be more wrong. The true adventure was just beginning.

Lewis had passed the winter and spring in northern New Mexico and eastern Colorado. There he had hunted big game on the plains and in the mountains. He had gotten to know the characters who peopled the Far West. During the spring he had witnessed the trials and executions of the ringleaders of the so-called Taos Pueblo Revolt. It had been his good luck to be befriended by a Cheyenne trader called Blackfoot John Smith. Smith took Lewis along with him as he circulated among the Indians. The winter he had spent much more enjoyably than witnessing the aftermath of the Taos Revolt. He spent those cold months in the teepees of the Cheyenne Indians on the plains of eastern Colorado. There he developed an appreciation for the total freedom of the life of the Plains Indians. But now Lewis was traveling with a wagon train. They were creeping east across the plains, going back home to what was called "the States." Smith, his Cheyenne wife, and infant son, Jack, also accompanied the wagon train. It was inching its way, at fifteen miles a day, east along the Arkansas River when the wagon train encountered Fort Mann, near present-day Dodge City, Kansas.

This location was approximately halfway between Santa Fe and Westport. Its midway location made the area one of concern for U.S. armed forces. An army presence would be found here, on and off, throughout most of the six decades of the Santa Fe Trail. It started with the patrol of Major Bennet Riley. He escorted the 1829 caravan to the Arkansas and waited with his troops over the summer. They camped west of present-day Lakin, Kansas. Riley and his men accompanied the returning traders back to Missouri. Another reason the area was of interest to the military was that it lay smack in the heart of the country claimed by the marauding Comanche and Kiowa Indians. The Pawnees also hunted (and raided) in the territory. All this made the region arguably the most dangerous on the entire length of the Santa Fe Trail, as was certainly the case in 1847 when Lewis and Smith and others approached the fort.

Fort Mann, established in 1846, amounted to four log shacks set in a square a hundred yards from the Arkansas River. A tall log fence, or palisade, surrounded the shanties, with no more than sixty feet separating the corner posts. Because it was meant to be a quartermaster's safe haven for wagon trains, the fort was manned by teamsters hired by the army. On the approach of Lewis's wagon train, the forty teamsters at the post set off the alarm. They scrambled inside and barred the gate. From the walkway along the top of the palisade, every man kept a close watch on the approaching wagons, which at first they mistakenly thought were Indians.

Just six days before, one of the teamsters had ventured down to the river. He wanted to relieve the dreary salt pork diet with some fresh catfish. Although he was no more than three hundred yards from the fort, a raiding party of Comanche bore down on him. While the teamsters on the fort's walls watched in horror, the man was lanced by the warriors on horseback, and his bloody scalp was pulled from his head. A warrior shook the "reeking scalp" at the men in the fort. He whooped with joy, and then, unscathed, the Indians dashed away.

Although not as tragic, another incident had occurred two days later. It showed the impotence of the teamsters. A party of Indians charged within seventy-five yards of the fort. This time they were after the fort's stock. Thirty oxen and forty mules were driven off. The men in the fort, safe behind the log palisade, blazed away at the Indians. One raider was shot off his horse. Two of his comrades, braving gunfire, ran their horses on either side of the fallen warrior. They swooped him up and bore him away at a fast gallop.

Traveling with Lewis's wagon train was a Captain A. W. Enos, who was in command of the fort. When the men at the post presented themselves, he was quickly informed of their opinion of the situation. "We don't care to stay here on fat pork and be scalped by Indians," they said. After much persuasion—and the offer of an additional $10 in salary, bringing their wages to $30 a month—nine agreed to remain. The new commander was to be Lewis's old friend, Blackfoot John Smith. So Lewis, for the sake of excitement, decided to remain. Captain Enos and other experienced plainsmen tried to talk young Lewis out of this decision. But Lewis wanted to experience an Indian fight. He stayed.

The men in the wagon train hitched up and rolled on. A feeling of immense loneliness and dread came over young Lewis. A visit to the river for water required a bucket in one hand and a gun in the other. The defenders called the fort the "Prairie Prison."

Lewis settled into the dreary, boring routine of post life. During the days he and the others carried adobe bricks, fortunately already made, into the fort. They built chimneys and fireproofed the roofs of the cabins. At night Smith detailed the men into watches. For two hours the two-man teams would peer into the night, listening for any stray sound, while coyotes skulked around the palings. Wolves scratched up and devoured the corpse of the luckless fisherman.

The few horses in the fort had consumed the grass near the buildings. One day Lewis took them a half mile away to graze. Suddenly, a gun was heard, the sign for danger. Lewis jumped bareback on the nearest animal. His good horse, Diabolique, broke away and scattered for the horizon. *There goes $80,* Lewis thought, not daring to try to chase after the horse. His hat flew from his head. On he rode, the rest of the herd fleeing with him. He tore through the portal of the fort, and the log gates, creaking on their wooden hinges, shrieked shut. In the distance the dust cloud that occasioned the scare became visible. It was a herd of wild horses.

Shortly, the real thing was upon them. A group of Indians were spotted trying to drive off the fort's small horse herd. All the men stood in the open gate. Seeing this, the Indians bore down on the men. At this point the men shifted, and the Indians noticed one of the fort's six-pound cannons was trained on them. They broke for cover with the makeshift force's rifle balls whizzing around them. The men purposefully aimed wide of the mark, not wanting to stir up any need for revenge on the Indians' part.

So matters continued for the better part of a month and a half. Wagon trains rolled up to the fort, many with woeful tales of Indian attack. Blackfoot Smith, seeing the utter foolhardiness of being a sitting duck, resigned his commission. He departed with a wagon train, urging Lewis to come along with him. The leader of the caravan, Ceran St. Vrain, also begged Lewis to return to the States. Lewis withstood their entreaties, but sometime later a friend of his father's, a Colonel Russell, rode into the fort. He absolutely refused to allow the youth, who had just turned eighteen, to remain in such dangerous territory.

The return trip to Missouri, however, proved far from uneventful. Colonel Russell's troop numbered eight-five men. The wagons tracked in a double file. At the threat of danger, they could corral easily. Toward the end of the first day's march, a guard hollered, "Injuns." The wagons circled around the crest of a little hill. The stock was driven inside the oval, and the men with firearms—believe it or not, thirty had none—stood outside the corral. The Indians charged furiously, riding around the wagons, brandishing their guns, screaming fiercely, their stout rawhide shields shifting continually to protect them from view of the teamsters.

Half the wagoners would fire, while the others stood by with loaded weapons. After several volleys the teamsters pulled back inside the wagons and "it became exciting. The warriors galloped furiously, bent down, now on this side, now on that, until nothing of their person could be seen, but the heel and part of the leg thrown across the cantle of the saddle. From under the horse's neck would issue a smoke cloud, as we heard the sighing of a ball as it cut its way overhead. Sharply sighted rifles gave ready answer, cheers rang out from our exhilarated party, and unfortunate oxen stung by furrowing bullets from lumbering escopetas [shotguns], plunged and horned each other from side to side of the crowded corral." After an hour the Indians melted away to the west, and the teamsters made for a better camping spot near water.

A couple of days later near the dreaded Coon Creeks region, Louis, Colonel Russell, and a trader named Coolidge rode away from the train to collect wood for their noon cup of coffee. Suddenly they noticed another party of wood gathers galloping pell-mell past them.

They pointed toward the wagon train. A force of Indians was endeavoring to cut the wood gatherers off from the caravan. Lewis had a fleet mount. It went even faster than the colonel's horse. Off he streaked toward the safety of the corralling wagons. But poor Coolidge, on a slow mule, fell farther and farther back. When within a safe distance of the corral, Lewis looked back and saw, to his horror, that the Indians were bearing down fast on Coolidge. He shouted to the colonel. The latter reined his horse in, fired a wide shot, and galloped for the corral. Lewis's animal, contrary to all expectations, stood stock still. Lewis drew a bead on the closest pursuer. He fired. The warrior was hit, and his horse turned and ran for the river. The example of the fallen warrior slowed those following him. Coolidge and Lewis both made it safely inside the corral, but the battle went on for hours.

Lewis's adventure on the Santa Fe Trail was not yet complete, and the worst was yet to come. A couple of days later, the Indians attacked yet again. This time, in a half hour's attack, the train lost 160 oxen, leaving the wagons almost immobile. Twenty-six wagons and any amount of supplies were left to the wolves and the Indians.

After all of his adventures, Lewis returned safely to Cincinnati. By 1850, when he was just twenty going on twenty-one, he had written and published an account of his ten months in the West. Called *Wah-to-yah and the Taos Trail,* the book ranks as one of the very best accounts of life in the mountains and plains ever written. Little wonder, given all he saw and did.

A SAPPINGTON FAMILY DINNER

- 1849 -

THE GREAT HOUSE, NAMED PRAIRIE PARK, looked as if it belonged somewhere in the plantation belt of the Deep South, standing two stories tall with gleaming white columns rising on either side of the front stoop. Inside on this fateful day in 1849, three of the most important men in Missouri politics were dining from the finest European china and silverware. The men were connected by marriage. Both of the younger men, Meredith Marmaduke, former governor, and Claiborne Jackson, a future governor, had married daughters of the family patriarch, Dr. John Sappington.

For a time John Sappington attended what is now the University of Pennsylvania medical school. He did not graduate, however, only took some medical courses. Many in his day adopted titles by practical experience. Today, few would doubt he wrote an important medical book. Many call it the most important early medical book published in the West. But in his day he was denounced as a quack. The medical wisdom of the time held that disease was caused by the body's "humors" getting out of sorts. The proper tools for a physician were believed to be a dreadful chest of lancets, blistering plasters, and occasionally even leeches. These gruesome implements were used to bleed patients or make them vomit. The theory went back to the Middle Ages. These practices often did more harm than good.

Malaria is probably the deadliest disease, on the basis of the number of people killed, in history. It fell into a group of generally unidentifiable diseases: fever, bilious fever, ague, chilblains, and so on. It was also the deadliest disease in early-day Missouri and along the Santa Fe Trail. In the 1600s explorers discovered what locals in South America had known for a long time, that the bark of a particular tree would help people with the deadly fever. The substance was taken back to Europe and became known as Peruvian bark. Later, in the early 1800s, two French scientists isolated quinine from the bark. Until the twentieth century quinine was one of a handful of effective treatments that medical science had developed.

It is well known today that malaria is transmitted by mosquitoes. But in trail days the general belief was that it was caused by exposure to night vapors or "bad air." This misconception led to the belief that tobacco smoke inoculated the smoker. Mosquitoes were especially troublesome along the eastern portions of the trail. But they could be encountered anywhere that water stood for a few days.

Dr. Sappington became the largest American importer of quinine. Single orders were sometimes as large as a quarter ton. Each pill contained one grain of quinine and enough licorice and gum myrrh to kill the bitter aftertaste. Sappington became rich. But many doctors decried his pills. They did not believe a patented medicine could be effective. He was denied admittance to the Missouri Medical Society. But the general public had much less doubt, and twenty-five workers were kept busy rolling Sappington's Anti-Fever Pills. During his lifetime about a million boxes of pills, at about $1.50 a box, were sold. Dr. Sappington's medication was probably the most widespread, effective patented medicine in the United States.

Son-in-law, Meredith Marmaduke, was born in Virginia in 1791. Marmaduke served as an officer in his home state during the War of 1812 and then moved to Missouri in 1824. One of the early Santa Fe traders, he married Lavinia Sappington and settled down to working with the doctor. He helped run a store and farmed on a large scale. He also engaged in politics and social projects. Perhaps the event that made him governor motivated his interest in social issues.

While Marmaduke was lieutenant governor, one morning Governor Thomas Reynolds ate a quiet breakfast, then went into another room and shot himself to death. One of Marmaduke's last acts as governor was proposing that the state establish a lunatic asylum. Like his father-in-law he was a leading member of Missouri's Inner Clique, the name given to those who supported Senator Thomas Hart Benton, one of the most powerful men in the U.S. government. A strong ally of Old Hickory, President Andrew Jackson, Benton believed in the western expansion of the United States. He thought homesteaders should be encouraged to settle the new western territories.

The other son-in-law, Claiborne Jackson, was younger than Governor Marmaduke by fifteen years. But he would not admit to being his inferior. He had been an infantry captain in the Black Hawk War in the 1830s. After that he sold Dr. Sappington's Anti-Fever Pills and served for twelve years in the state legislature, including two years as speaker, a position almost as powerful as that of acting governor. Now as the three men ate dinner in the late 1840s, the political climate had undergone a wrenching change. The leader of the Democratic Party, Thomas Hart Benton, was wobbling on one of the bedrock positions of the party. Though a plantation owner and slave owner himself, Benton was beginning to disavow the practice of slavery.

All of the men at that family dinner at Prairie Park owned slaves. As strange as it may seem, Dr. Sappington held enlightened medical views but medieval social ones. Slaves were the workforce rolling Sappington's Anti-Fever Pills. Marmaduke backed Benton. He believed slavery was an outdated social custom. He felt it had to go. Sappington and Jackson opposed this view.

Though the three men, Sappington, Marmaduke, and Jackson managed to remain civil, their political differences could not help but cause a fracture. Marmaduke and Sappington curtailed their joint business ventures. From then on, Dr. Sappington favored Jackson. And for the moment Sappington and Jackson seemed to win. Benton was defeated in his bid for a sixth term as senator.

But in the end none of these men won. At the outbreak of the Civil War, Jackson, then governor of Missouri, tried to lead the state into the Confederacy. But Missouri legislators refused to secede. Ultimately, he became Confederate governor in exile in Arkansas. Four of Marmaduke's sons fought for the Confederacy, two of them being killed in battle. Marmaduke, a staunch Unionist to the end, died of natural causes during the war. No doubt his heart was broken too by the tragedy of war. His son, John Sappington Marmaduke, became the first former Confederate elected governor of Missouri in 1884. In one way he was true to his father's vision. He promoted social causes such as better schools and curbing the predatory practices of the railroads, which took advantage of the small farmer.

Today, all three of the men who suffered through those tense times in Missouri's Little Dixie, from 1849 through the Civil War, lie buried together in the same cemetery, the Sappington family burial ground, not far from the prewar mansion of Prairie Park.

A WINTER CROSSING OF THE PRAIRIE

- 1852 -

THE OLD-TIMERS AT INDEPENDENCE SHOOK THEIR HEADS. A mere eighteen men, three wagons, and three carriages—with three women and two children—were going to brave the plains? The caravan was not large enough to brave an attack. But even worse was the month—October. It was madness. They would all be lost.

But Dr. Michael Steck did not listen. He had been appointed as agent for the Mescalero Apaches in New Mexico. Duty called, and he proposed to go. The first couple of days on the trail were great fun. Dr. Michael shot prairie chickens and personally supervised their cooking. Then it began to rain. And it rained, all the way to Council Grove, where they arrived in about a week.

The Kanza Indian agency was situated at Council Grove, and at this time of year, the tribe drew annual rations. The Kanza performed the buffalo dance, which amused Dr. Michael and company. But the festivities soon turned dark when some young men arrived, riding dramatically through the mud streets of the prairie village. On a lance one carried the scalp of their foe, a Shawnee, making for great excitement and cheering on the part of the Indians, and a scalp dance was performed.

The next day Dr. Michael and his party left Council Grove, happy to be away from the "civilized" Kanza Indians. That afternoon in the hills west of the village, a prairie thunderstorm caught them. Bolts of lightning electrified the gloomy afternoon. Peels of thunder echoed off the hills and rolled down the valleys as buckets of water cascaded out of the sky. The mules had better sense than their drivers. They refused to go on, turning their rumps into the storm. The humans huddled in their carriages and wagons, eating cold meat and hardtack for supper. By nightfall the wind dropped, and they pitched tents. Though there was no wood for a fire to warm them, they slept soundly. The next day, though still traveling in rain, they headed for the next good camping spot, Cottonwood Creek, twenty miles away. The trail had been churned to peanut butter by the rains, but they slogged on. Dark came, and every lurch threatened to dump a vehicle into a gully. They kept on, arriving at the creek about eight in the evening. After chores, which included picketing the animals, gathering firewood, and cooking supper, a meal was ready to eat by eleven at night.

All this called for a little rest and some thanksgiving. Ducks and turkeys were shot and roasted. The following day Dr. Michael and company trekked to Big Turkey Creek. Dr. Michael sensed danger. A spot was seen moving on the prairie, soon identified as an Indian. Since they were still in Osage territory, an attack was unlikely, but the theft of their mules was possible. In such situations the Osage usually pretended to have found "strayed" animals and offered to give them back—for a reward. But the men took no chances. They were on the edge of the plains. The loss of the animals, especially with winter approaching, could be disastrous. They posted a double guard.

Dr. Michael had been right in his belief danger was at hand. But it didn't come from the Indians. The next afternoon it began to snow. This was not the puffy, white, Christmas kind of snowfalls he had come to expect in Pennsylvania. This was a plains snowstorm with strong winds. They were on the high prairie with not a stick of wood in sight. Four inches of snow was on the ground and the trail ruts were filling. When the ruts were completely obscured, they'd be lost. Then suddenly as all hope seemed lost, the sun came out. It quit snowing, and before them was the Little Arkansas with plentiful wood and a good camping spot. Disaster had been averted.

They pressed on. Now it was very cold, but that slight inconvenience was made up for by entering the buffalo range. Fresh meat was at hand. That was good. Not so good was the band of forty-five Osage hunters they encountered. As allies of the white man, the Osage crowded into camp and pressed the demands of friendship. Dr. Michael was afraid their mules were about to be stolen. Then worse, ahead more men on horseback were spotted. But these turned out to be a company of dragoons from Fort Atkinson (near present-day Dodge City). The Indians left but now another storm threatened. However, this time they knew what to do. Some gathered wood, others picketed the animals in sheltered locations, and yet others reinforced the tent ropes.

The next morning, despite the storm, they were up early. They trekked along the Arkansas River. It continued being excessively cold. Buffalo were everywhere, and so were wolves. Sometimes as many as fifty wolves would be seen at the same time. Whenever one pressed too close to the caravan, it would be shot. On the fourth day they reached Fort Atkinson. Because of the women and children in the party, the officers treated them kindly, but after two days Dr. Michael resumed his march along the river. Snow on the upland prairie drove the buffalo down along the river. It seemed as though the vast buffalo herd had to be parted to allow passage of the small wagon train.

Quicksand bogged down one of the wagons a hundred yards from shore when they were crossing the Arkansas. They had to wade the river in the freezing cold, unloading the contents by hand. Finally, the wagon was extracted, and they headed southwest across the Cimarron Desert. Dr. Michael's band made twenty-two miles to Bear Creek. Digging in the bed of the creek did not produce water. They were by no means sure any would be found the next day either, when someone remembered spying a snowbank a few miles back, and men were sent to retrieve some snow. Just enough fuel was found to melt the water. Everyone received a cup of coffee and the animals were given a quart of water a piece.

The night was dark and stormy. As it progressed, snow began to fall and it became much, much colder. The mules, on their picket ropes, started shivering. That was a bad sign. The Cimarron Desert was known for terrible blizzards that killed stock. A trader by the name of Albert Speyer had lost 175 animals not far from that very spot just five years before. The skulls of the animals could still be seen on the side of the trail. The men unrolled themselves from their blankets and took their covers and wrapped them around the animals.

Returning to the tent, they amused themselves with stories of freighters lost in blizzards on the plains. One of them told about the wagon train that lost two hundred mules just the winter before and described how two of the men who tried to walk out froze to death. About two o'clock in the morning, the snow on the tent became too heavy. The guy ropes pulled out and the frozen fabric collapsed on those inside. The folks had a good laugh about this. They decided to leave the tent as it was. The snow acted as insulation, and so while others talked, Dr. Michael thought back to the delicacy one of the old trappers with them had cooked up a few days before. He had taken a buffalo calf's head, dug a hole, placed rocks in the bottom, and then poured coals from a fire on top. The calf's head was placed in the hole. More coals were added and the hole was covered. Breakfast the next morning was an untold delight, baked calf's head. Clearly, the men (and women and children) who braved the Santa Fe Trail were hearty and adventurous folk.

Dr. Michael and his family defied initial expectations and succeeded in their crossing of the plains. Once safely ensconced in New Mexico, he found the job as Indian agent immensely satisfying—and the Mescalero Apache thought he was a good agent. During the Civil War, when military rule was the order of the day, Dr. Steck stood up for the Indians, earning the condemnation of many whites but the gratitude of his Apache wards. Much later, long after the Civil War, he returned to Pennsylvania and spent his last days in the state of his youth.

SATANK SHOOTS A PEACOCK
OFF THE ROOF

- 1860 -

IN EARLY SEPTEMBER OF 1860, SATANK, a Kiowa war chief with a number of warriors, rode up to Walnut Creek Trading Ranch on the Santa Fe Trail. Satank was about fifty years old, and he was known as a particularly wily leader of an unusually clever and brave tribe of Indians.

Walnut Creek, 125 miles from Council Grove, became the site of the first trading post on the Santa Fe Trail past the famous outpost. Council Grove, where the wagons formed into wagon trains, was almost completely safe from Indian attack. The Walnut Creek area, on the other hand, lay in the heart of the most dangerous section for much of the trail's sixty years. The trading post had been built in 1855 by William Allison and Francis Booth, both rough and tough frontiersmen. They had been heading to the gold diggings farther west, but their wagons broke down near Walnut Creek. The spot looked like a fine place for a trading post, and they proceeded to make one there.

The creek provided plenty of timber for the kind of fortified building required in such a turbulent area. They cut logs, built a crude cabin, and fenced in about an acre of ground. A narrow trading window was built into the cabin, with a drop door of heavy logs suspended above it. In case of trouble a quick twist of a rope sprung the door, slamming it down and securing the store. Some accounts say parts of the edifice were constructed of stone or sod. Others say the entire structure, including the trading post/house itself, was of logs set upright. Everyone agrees there was an observation tower on the roof of the cabin. In wild country such as this, one had always to be on the lookout. Should unknown men approach, the gates and trading window could be secured. A relatively small number inside could fend off a much larger force outside. In turbulent times the observation tower was manned day and night.

Life at Walnut Creek Trading Ranch, though dangerous, turned a profit. In their very first months, Allison and Booth, according to a New York newspaper, "returned to Independence, Mo., from the Plains, where they have been for some weeks on a buffalo hunt. The party brought in over 10,000 pounds of dried buffalo meat and tongues. They killed over 50 buffalo and more than 200 wolves."

That winter, the first for the trading post on Walnut Creek, was a rugged one. The Arkansas River, only a few miles away, froze to the bottom. Snow was so deep on the plains the mail stage quit running. But those who did brave the trail stopped at the Walnut Creek Station, making the new enterprise even more profitable. Newspapers in the Kansas City area sung the praises of the new trading post. The *Occidental Messenger* said:

> *This [trading ranch] is the first attempt at building by citizens made West of Council Grove, and we hope it may grow up in a short time [into] a flourishing settlement. The men at the head of this enterprise are well known here, and distinguished for their energy and*

determination. They have no fear about them. This set-
tlement will be another stopping point on the route to
New Mexico, and will make, in a little while, the road
less dangerous, by lessening the distance between civi-
lized points and affording those in danger or want an
opportunity to obtain relief.

Not surprisingly, the early views of success were too optimistic. First, Allison lost the post office contract. Not enough mail was sent to or from that outpost on the plains to justify paying a postmaster. Then, more ominously, Booth was killed in a rather gruesome way: "The [man] who brutally murdered Mr. Booth at Walnut Creek, last month, by splitting his head open with an ax, was arrested in San Miguel county [New Mexico] last week."

Allison sold out to a man named George Peacock. Like Allison and Booth, Peacock had extensive experience in the West. He had panned for gold for a time in California before returning to the plains where he managed the mule herd of an expedition crossing the prairie.

One day in the late summer of 1860, Satank told Peacock he thought some troops were coming from Pawnee Rock. He implored him to take his telescope to the observation tower to find out. There was urgency in his voice. It was entirely possible the troops were looking for Satank for some infraction or another. Just a few days earlier, a detail of soldiers had attempted to arrest him. But the trader had intervened. The war chief remained free.

The trader obliged Satank. Not much harm could come of it, he thought. There were two other men inside the fortified trading ranch. One was a German immigrant, universally called a Dutchman, by the name of Myers. The other was a Mexican herder. A third man lay ill in his bed and would have been of no help in a brawl. But the trader expected no trouble as he climbed to the roof to have a look.

It was Peacock whom Satank asked to climb the observation tower. From the top of the post buildings, he looked for the troop of soldiers from Pawnee Rock. His telescope showed no soldiers coming his way, nor did it spot a cloud of dust from horses' hooves. However, looking down at Satank on the ground outside the wall of the trading post, he saw something that made his blood run cold. The old war chief was training his rifle on Peacock himself. "Satank, you damned son of a bitch," Peacock cursed. Those were his last words. Satank's gun let out a boom, and Peacock was shot through the temple. He fell dead. Satank's braves stormed the fort, killing Myers and the herder. The sick man rolled up in his blankets and was left unharmed. The Indians then looted the post.

But do not judge Satank's actions too quickly. He had his reasons. Indians frequently carried letters of reference from white friends. These letters would say that they were friendly to whites and that they should be treated kindly. That spring, Satank had appealed to George Peacock, who he felt was his friend, for such a letter. Peacock provided one. It read, Satank is "the dirtiest, laziest, lousiest vagabond on the plains. If he comes to your camp, kick him out."

George Peacock had a good laugh at Satank's expense.

But Satank had the last laugh. Among his last acts in the sacking of the trading post was climbing the roof to mutilate Peacock's body. He tore the hair from the dead man's head and rode off onto the prairie with George Peacock's scalp.

Perhaps because the trader had affronted Satank's dignity, military authorities seem not to have made a serious attempt to punish Satank, and he figured prominently at the Medicine Lodge treaty seven years later. But in 1871 Satank was arrested by soldiers in Oklahoma. He was believed to be behind the attack on a wagon train in Texas in which seven men were killed. Shot trying to escape, Satank was buried in the military cemetery at Fort Sill, Oklahoma.

A NIGHT RIDE
ON THE SANTA FE TRAIL

- 1862 -

MOST TRAVELED THE SANTA FE TRAIL BY DAYLIGHT. But some whose business was not on the up-and-up moved along the trail at night. During the tense times known as Bleeding Kansas in the late 1850s, and during the Civil War in the early 1860s, many more rode the trail at night

Just before the Fourth of July 1862, William "Bill" Anderson, his brother James, or more commonly Jim, and at least one other man set out from Missouri on a small expedition down the trail. In the dark of the moon, they sneaked by the guard posts of Union soldiers on the Kansas border and made their way to the trail and headed west. Come morning they sought refuge in groves of trees or at the houses of Southern sympathizers. But by 1862 there were not many Southern sympathizers left in Kansas. Most of them had been run out of the state by "Jayhawkers," bands of Free State partisans who treated roughly those who wanted Kansas to be a slave state.

Bill and Jim traveled for several nights. They ended up more than 120 miles into Kansas, in the area known as the Flint Hills, a gorgeous rolling country with tall grass on the hilltops and densely wooded watercourses. At this early date only the country near the trail was settled. On their last night of travel, they held up in some trees on Bluff Creek. Not far away lay a burnt-out homestead, one Bill and Jim found very familiar. The owner had eked out a living selling produce and other articles to the teamsters on the trail. The "trading ranch," as it was known, had been torched because it belonged to Sesesh sympathizers. Seeing the burned-out buildings filled Bill and Jim's hearts with rage. This farmstead had been their family home until their father was murdered trying to defend their sister's honor and they were hounded from the country.

Their father, William Sr., like many who lived or worked on the Santa Fe Trail, was born in Kentucky. As a young man he drifted to Missouri, where he married and had six children. He left his wife and family, seeking his fortune in the California goldfields. Not finding it there, he returned to Missouri and started over again on Bluff Creek in the Flint Hills. His son Bill hired out for a couple of years to a nearby rancher, who described him as a "good boy, steady as a clock." Upon reaching twenty-one, Bill homesteaded a claim to gain some property. In the months when the farm work didn't require his presence, he traveled across the plains to Santa Fe as a hand. When he worked his way up to second boss, he figured out where the real money lay. Returning shortly after setting out on the trail with a wagon train, Bill Jr. and the trail boss claimed they "lost" the train because the stock had strayed. There was nothing to do but accept their word. But skeptics weren't greatly surprised to find young Bill following Arthur I. Baker into Missouri on a expedition to plunder wealthy farmers.

Baker also ran a trading ranch on Rock Creek a few miles west of the Anderson. He named his little station rather grandly, Agnes City, after his mother. At first, in the mid-1850s, times were good. Then drought struck. Crops failed. To compensate himself for this bad luck, Baker led raids, like the one Bill was now on, far away across the border into Missouri. From their base more than a hundred miles inside Kansas, they continued making forays into the Show Me State. Showing a glimmer of Southern patriotism, young Bill's preferred targets seem to have been Unionists. But, all in all, he acted without prejudice, Jayhawking pro-Confederates or bushwhacking Federal sympathizers. Young Bill once told a friend, "I don't care any more for the South than you."

All that abruptly changed when Baker made eyes at Bill's fifteen-year-old sister, Mary Ellen. The family was happy to have such a leading citizen marry into it. But then the rascal Baker proceeded to engage himself to another. On top of this, he had the gall to take back two horses stolen by one of Bill's gang. Baker then swore out a warrant for the man's arrest. William Anderson Sr. showed true Southern dudgeon. He fortified himself with a belt of corn liquor. He grabbed his shotgun and rode the five miles to Agnes City. Had he proceeded at that point to Baker's house, things may have turned out differently. But first he decided to have a snort at Baker's store. While William Sr. was nipping at the jug, a bystander removed the caps from his gun. When the older Anderson then burst into Baker's home and rampaged up the steps, he was met with a blast of Baker's own scattergun. He was killed instantly. Bill and Jim fled immediately to Missouri, later sending a man to retrieve their three sisters.

And now they were back on Bluff Creek. Instead of riding right into Agnes City and confronting Baker, they had a friend go to Baker's house. It was late. Baker was suspicious. The excuse the Anderson boys' accomplice made was that he wanted to buy whiskey for a nearby wagon train. He claimed that the teamsters wanted to properly anoint the Fourth of July. Having descended into the basement storeroom, Baker looked up and saw Bill and Jim Anderson. He went for the pistols strapped to his belt. His shot hit Jim in the thigh, but Bill's aim was true. It slammed Baker to the basement floor. Leaving him moaning, the Anderson boys piled kegs on top of the trapdoor and set the store ablaze. They knew that Baker, who was a huge man, was too hefty to scramble through the basement window. They waited until they heard a shot indicating Baker had killed himself to keep from burning alive.

Grimly satisfied, they hightailed it ahead of an enraged posse up the Santa Fe Trail to safety in Missouri, stealing a change of mounts at each stage station. But the older Anderson boy, who came to be known as Bloody Bill Anderson, was not through with the Santa Fe Trail. He rode with Dick Yager (sometime spelled Yeager) on a raid along the trail even deeper into Kansas the following year. And he also became one of the most notorious of Quantrill's Raiders, who took the trail on their infamous raid on Lawrence. On another occasion he was known to have attacked and destroyed a bull train just inside Kansas. Maybe after the bad things that happened to his family on the trail, he detested both the trail and everyone who worked it. Or maybe it was just that Santa Fe–bound trains were where the easy money was.

PRAIRIE FIRE

- 1861 -

LYDIA SPENCER LANE HAD EXPERIENCED A PRAIRIE FIRE on the Santa
Fe Trail before. On that hot July day, the grass just outside the circled
wagons ignited. In her tent when the alarm went up and only in her
undergarments, she left her valuables, wedding ring, jewelry, and so on,
and hurriedly struggled into her hoopskirt dress and grabbed the baby.
She fled outside and watched as the soldiers—she was an officer's wife
and she was traveling with a military caravan—extinguished the blaze.
It was very hot. Not a breeze was stirring, very unusual for the plains
of Kansas. Wet gunnysacks (burlap bags) were all that it took to put
out the fire. Lydia's tent wasn't even much affected. A few tent stakes
had been scorched. That was all. These prairie fires weren't all that big
of a deal—at least that one wasn't.

Lydia, as an officer's wife, was used to braving frontier conditions, and her background suited her for such a life. Although her
father was Major George Blaney of the U.S. Engineer Corps stationed in Carlisle, Pennsylvania, Lydia was born on civilian ground

because her father died before she came into the world, in 1835. Although she never knew her father or camp life with her family, she married an officer stationed at Carlisle Barracks, William Bartlett Lane. Lane was a mustang, a man who came up from the ranks being commissioned during the Mexican-American War.

Lydia's first experience as an army bride was a posting to the frontier in Texas. The arduous passage to Galveston took two weeks by ship, with "only one death." She arrived in Corpus Christi in the middle of a yellow fever epidemic, with nothing but a tent on the beach for quarters. A "blue norther" cold snap ended the threat of yellow fever but almost blew Lydia's tent—with her in it—into the gulf. Finally, orders were cut for her husband. He was to be posted near the Rio Grande far to the west of San Antonio. A military caravan headed inland. The army officially made no provision for officers' wives. So far as the armed services were concerned, they did not exist. The only women officially countenanced on an army post were laundresses. Nevertheless, an ambulance, that is, a carriage for several people, was furnished for the wives and children, and it was loaded to the gills. The other wives were stout, and their husbands outranked Lydia's. Their children were also plentiful. Lydia had only a small spot on which to sit. Whenever an item was needed, the wives expected her to rush about finding it. Her first house at Fort Inge, Texas, a dilapidated log cabin, was just a bit better than the tent on the beach at Corpus Christi. In spite of all, Lydia found the trip, and camp life, exciting. She was entranced by her new surroundings on the frontier, and she especially liked the culture of the Mexican people, whom she found all about.

But Lydia's experience had fooled her on one score. Prairie fires were much more serious than she believed. This time it wasn't the middle of summer. Rather it was late in the fall, and the Kansas winds were blowing. Fine grit hung suspended or rather moving along with the breeze, making the air seem like very fine sandpaper. And it was cold. Lydia was again moving across the state with a wagon train and children. The fort her husband had been stationed at, Fort Fillmore, in New Mexico, just north of El Paso, had been attacked by Confederate forces from west Texas. It seemed certain the Confederates would march up the Rio Grande valley in an attempt to capture New Mexico. Noncombatants were ordered back to the States, so Lydia and her family found themselves shivering and frigid on the Santa Fe Trail two weeks out from Fort Leavenworth. Lydia looked forward to creeping inside her tent and snuggling up in her bed robes.

One thing she didn't like was the site of the camp selected by Captain Joseph Potter, who was in command of the train. The camp was situated on a bluff overlooking a creek with tall grass all about. Frost had struck, and the grass was brittle and dry, highly flammable. Lydia didn't like the idea of campfires all around and so much tinder about. She informed Captain Potter of this fact, but coming from a woman, her opinion was dismissed. He told her that if a fire should start, the wind would blow it away from the camp. He was certain. Lydia, a twenty-six-year-old army wife, had already crossed the plains on the Santa Fe Trail several times. But Potter was a captain. He must know what he was talking about.

Camp was pitched. The tent was up and the camp furniture was placed inside. The cots were erected and the bedclothes were spread on them. Lydia had just gone inside when she heard an enormous roaring. She'd never heard anything like that before and knew it was trouble. From the tent doorway she saw what was causing the awful sound.

The grass was ablaze. Wind-driven flames jumped a hundred feet at a time. And contrary to Captain Potter's assurances, they were heading right toward her. It was impossible to fight this fire with wet burlap bags. The only thing to do was run. She darted inside the tent and gathered up what clothes she could manage, grabbed her two children by their arms, and fled. The servants followed. Outside, in the cold, she saw the other army wives with their children. Lydia instructed them to make for the creek below the bluff. That was their only hope. They ran down the slope, into the knee-deep creek. The children splashed through the water, wetting themselves to their chests. On the far bank, the women and children watched the officers and men try to put out the fire. They beat at it with whatever they had at hand, mostly blankets. Some took off their coats and used them. It was no use. This fire could not be contained. After a while the officers crossed the creek. Where the women and children were watching the blaze was not entirely safe because the wind-driven fire could possibly jump the stream, so the officers led the women down to a bend in the creek, which was safer—for the moment. They must have wondered how they could possibly survive two more weeks on the trail in freezing cold weather without their camping gear.

A soldier had accidentally started the prairie fire. Bothered by the weeds behind his campsite, he threw a match in them, with the wind at his back. In an instant the weeds were gone, and the flames were racing across the tallgrass toward Lydia's camp. When she returned, she found only the iron ends of the tent poles. The cots, table, chairs, lunch chest, and blankets had burned to a powder. The large carriage in which Lydia and the children had ridden was also gone. Only the iron running gear remained. Inside the carriage had been stored extra coats, caps, shawls, and other articles of clothing, but they had gone up in smoke too.

Although others lost some things, Lydia's camp was hit the worst by the thoughtless soldier's actions. The commissary train was alright. And so the army took care of Lydia and her children on the final two-week leg of the journey. Well, not the army—the officers and men. A wall tent, called a Sibley tent, slept in by officers was given to Lydia for her family's use. The officers who vacated their comfortable tent moved into a three-man tent, already occupied by some officers. On the frontier—and among the armed services—folks looked out for each other. A couple of blankets had been saved, and there were some sheepskins to sleep on. A little coat was found for her son.

But one item was irreplaceable, a small leather trunk that contained her money and valuables. Had that burned up too? If so, Lydia would find herself in Fort Leavenworth completely destitute. But looking on the pile of blankets stowed in her new Sibley, Lydia spotted the chest. How had it gotten there? At once the mystery was solved. After she ran to the creek with the children, Neff, a manservant her husband had hired to help her cross the plains, had retrieved the chest from the tent and stuck around fighting the fire. Thanks to him, at least Lydia was not broke.

Lydia and her children endured the Civil War in Pennsylvania, after which her husband was again posted to New Mexico. Then suddenly in 1870, he was forced by ill health to retire from the military. During the fourteen years William Lane was married to Lydia and in the army, he was never posted in a single place more than six months, and she crossed the plains on the Santa Fe Trail seven times, as many as many grizzled old-timers. However, Lydia's last crossing of the plains was quite different from her first one. She traveled in a Pullman sleeper car on the transcontinental railroad.

MAJOR WYNKOOP'S NARROW ESCAPE

- 1864 -

FOR FIVE DAYS, STARTING ON SEPTEMBER 6, Major Edward Wynkoop directed his force of 127 mounted men across the short-grass prairie. They started from Fort Lyon on the mountain route of the Santa Fe Trail in southeastern Colorado and now were riding northeast across the plains. Along with the major's command rode four Cheyenne Indians. These Indians, including a chief called One Eye, supposedly were hostages. They came with the soldiers to show the good intentions of the Cheyenne. But Wynkoop had his doubts.

The unrelievedly flat countryside grew hilly as Wynkoop's men approached the Smoky Hill River. The detail had crossed the border into Kansas. Down in a slight valley, Wynkoop looked up to see a mass of Indian horsemen. Five to eight hundred of them were drawn up in a battle line, and they were well armed with bows, arrows, war lances, revolvers, and rifles. They raised their arms in a display of defiance. Wynkoop ordered his supply wagons into a circle. His mounted troopers were themselves formed into battle formation.

Major Wynkoop cursed himself. He told himself he should have known that he was being led into a trap. During the summer of 1864 the central plains smoldered with Indian trouble. In May the Cheyenne had killed a man at Cow Creek Station along the Santa Fe Trail far to the east in east central Kansas. Then the wily Kiowa chief Satanta raided the horse herd at Fort Larned. He decoyed the troopers by staging a dance performed by Kiowa women. While the entertainment was going on, he plundered the horse herd. A signal was given and the women slunk away and joined the fleeing Indians. Then on July Fourth wagon trains were besieged on Cow Creek. Afterward the Indians shifted their attentions to the Overland Trail along the Platte River in Nebraska, attacking wagon trains there and farms and ranches along the way. Several white women and children were taken captive. In August wagon trains were ravaged on the Santa Fe Trail in southwestern Kansas, with many teamsters killed. One entire train was lost when the mules were run off, the wagons burned, and the bodies of ten victims horribly mutilated. Although the culprits responsible for the latter attacks on the Santa Fe Trail were the notorious Kiowa and Comanche, many of the outrages over the summer had been committed by Cheyenne.

Then in September, three Indians, led by One Eye, rode into Fort Lyon on the mountain route of the Santa Fe Trail in eastern Colorado. They carried a letter, written in good English. The note said the Cheyenne wanted peace. The chief who signed the letter, Black Kettle, asked for a parley. As an added inducement, he said the Cheyenne had white captives they would like to trade. The lure of the white women and children captives was too much for Wynkoop to turn down. The deportment of the Cheyenne men who brought the letter further enticed the major. He found their demeanor very honorable. Chief One Eye said he would willingly risk death in order to bring about peace. Wynkoop was so impressed that though undermanned, he led his small detachment of troops off to talk to the Cheyenne.

And now here he was, frightfully outnumbered by at least five to one, and the warriors on the distant ridge were hollering and whooping it up. The hostage, One Eye, asked to go to them. Seeing no other alternative, Wynkoop let him go. Wynkoop was surprised (but pleased) when One Eye returned. He said Black Kettle would come to talk peace. Wynkoop withdrew his force eight miles to a better defensive position and waited for Black Kettle, all the while warriors circling his troops and chanting awful songs. Some said the chants were battle songs; others said they were simply cries for food. But either way, they put the soldiers on edge. In due time Black Kettle and the other chiefs galloped into Wynkoop's camp. They too were suspicious. Why had Wynkoop brought soldiers and a cannon if he wanted peace, they wanted to know. "Because of bad Indians," Wynkoop said. That made sense. No one knew better than the Cheyenne that the western plains were a dangerous place, and that there were plenty of "bad" men, on both sides.

One of the Cheyenne leaders, the tall, strong Bull Bear, spoke first. He said he thought there was no hope for peace between the whites and the Indians. One Eye stood and answered him. He said he was embarrassed that the Indians (meaning Bull Bear and his faction of Dog Soldiers) were making a big fuss about nothing more than a few horses. He offered to divide his herd with Bull Bear. Bull Bear, a tall commanding figure, accepted One Eye's horses and promptly departed. After that the talks went more smoothly.

Wynkoop said he wasn't a big enough chief to make a peace. But if the Cheyenne turned over the white captives they held, he would arrange for a powwow with the white chiefs in Denver. Black Kettle asked the white officer to wait while he tried to round up the hostages. Black Kettle and the other Cheyenne rode off, leaving Wynkoop's command to wait.

The soldiers in the ranks threatened mutiny. They thought they were sitting ducks. The Indians had just gone off to prepare themselves for battle, they told their commander. The Indians would return all right—but with guns blazing and arrows whistling.

But Major Wynkoop soothed them. He told them to be patient. It was in everyone's interest to give peace a chance. And to everyone's surprise—including probably Major Wynkoop's—a small delegation of Cheyenne rode peacefully into camp at noon on the second day. They were led by Arapaho ally, Chief Left Hand. With them was an adult woman captive, Laura Roper. He said Black Kettle would bring more captives the next day. Left Hand and the Indians with him offered to stay with the whites as hostages until Black Kettle appeared. The next day the chief appeared as promised. With him were three children who, along with Laura Roper, were captured on the Blue River in eastern Kansas. Black Kettle said there were other captives, two adult women and a child, but the Indians who held them would not give them up. He said it would require more diplomacy to retrieve them.

Major Wynkoop was very pleased with the upshot of this expedition. He had given peace a chance, and it seemed to work. He asked Black Kettle if he and a delegation of Cheyenne and Arapaho would go with him to Denver. They could present their case for peace to the governor of Colorado, the man who could make a binding treaty. Black Kettle said he had an American flag, presented to him by Abraham Lincoln in Washington, D.C. He said he would fly it over his teepee to show his friendship with the Americans. In his heart Major Wynkoop believed Black Kettle. Wynkoop, although relatively new as commander of Fort Lyon, had learned that the Southern Cheyenne, as opposed to those in Wyoming and Montana, had long been associated with Bent's Fort. William Bent had married a Cheyenne, and his sons, who had been educated in the East, lived with the Cheyenne. One had even written the letter signed by Black

Kettle that attracted Wynkoop to this powwow on the plains. The Cheyenne had been friendly to the Americans when all other tribes were on the warpath. The Arapaho, who were Cheyenne allies, were somewhat less friendly to the whites. But Wynkoop was willing to take Black Kettle's word that the Arapaho with him were also well disposed. The meeting ended with all satisfied. The Cheyenne chiefs would come to Fort Lyon, and then they and the officers from the fort would go to Denver to talk to the governor. Even Wynkoop's troopers were happy with the outcome. They had to agree that the major had taken a chance, and that it turned out well for all involved. The soldiers galloped across the plains to their fort. The Cheyenne returned to their village on the Smoky Hill and awaited the day for going to see the governor. Black Kettle flew the American flag given him by President Lincoln.

KIT CARSON AND THE FIRST BATTLE
OF ADOBE WALLS

- 1864 -

In November of 1864, Brigadier General James Carleton, commander of the department of New Mexico at Santa Fe, detailed Colonel Kit Carson to march east across the plains. His mission was to defeat the Kiowa, Kiowa-Apache, and Comanche. These southern Plains tribes had taken advantage of a United States military weakened by the Civil War. They had wreaked havoc on the Santa Fe Trail and outlying settlers in the region.

Kit Carson, then fifty-four years old, set out from Fort Bascom on the Canadian River in eastern New Mexico. His force, the First Cavalry, New Mexico volunteers, consisted of 14 officers and 321 enlisted men. Kit had also recruited an auxiliary force of seventy-five to a hundred Ute and Jicarilla fighters. Kit's ace in the hole was two lightweight howitzers. These guns, though slowing the column down, provided the key to preventing the forthcoming battle from becoming a disaster. General Carleton was right in sending Kit Carson, the renowned scout and mountain man, to find the Plains tribes. Kit found his Indians alright. What he discovered was similar to what Custer blundered into a dozen years later on the Little Bighorn. However, the mountain howitzers and Kit Carson's leadership proved to be the difference between the outcomes of these two battles with superior Indian forces.

Kit's command followed the Canadian River into the Texas panhandle. Evidently, Kit contemplated using an old outpost of Bent's Fort in northern Texas as his base of operations. Years before, when Kit had been hunter and all-round hand for the Bent brothers, he had worked at this post. It had been established for the convenience of the southern Plains tribes. Truthfully, the Bents had also desired to keep the Comanche and Kiowa away from Bent's Fort in Colorado. The Cheyenne and Arapaho routinely traded there, and those tribes didn't always get along well with the Comanche and Kiowa. Also, in the early days of the trail, the Comanche and Kiowa attacked wagon trains more often than the other tribes. After a few years the trading post, constructed of adobe, was abandoned. The subsequent landmark, in an area with few landmarks, became known as Adobe Walls. But Kit thought what was left of the post would provide some shelter from the notoriously harsh plains winter.

A snowstorm struck when Kit came within thirty miles of Adobe Walls. Indian scouts who braved the weather reported a large assemblage of Indians dead ahead at Adobe Walls. Leaving the baggage train under his second in command, Kit moved out during the night. He took only the mounted horsemen, including the Indian scouts and the howitzers. When within fifteen miles of the old fort, the column halted and awaited sunrise. No talking or fires were permitted. The night was uncomfortably cold. But all this just added to the element of surprise when in early morning his troops burst in upon the Kiowa camp of about 150 teepees.

The camp was that of the most respected chief of the Kiowa, To-hauson, an old man. Tragically, the section of the village first attacked housed the sick and the elderly, many of whom were the first to fall. Women and children scattered into the underbrush and across the broken hills of the Canadian River brakes. Among those secreted away was a white captive, Millie Durgan. Upon attack captives were usually killed, generally by jealous wives of the warriors who claimed them. During the early phase of the skirmish, Millie, however, was lucky to be allowed to hide away with the womenfolk and children. But would she be killed as she tried to sneak away to the troopers?

At the time a much more pressing question to Chief To-hauson was spreading the word of the attack. No more than a mile away lay a Comanche village of five hundred teepees. They had to be warned so their womenfolk and children could take cover and their warriors be brought into the battle. By some estimates as many as three to seven thousand Indians were camped in Canadian River valley. This time the whites, who had forted up in the ruins of Adobe Walls, could be annihilated.

The combined force of Indians fought brilliantly. Chief To-hauson's horse was shot out from under him. He continued the fight without flinching. He led charge after charge around the American position. Another chief, known as Stumbling Bear, had been given a special medicine shawl by his daughter. This shawl was supposed to protect him from white man's bullets. And it worked. Though the shawl was shot to pieces by Kit's force in the crumbling adobe walls, Stumbling Bear remained unscathed.

The notorious Chief Satanta had a few tricks up his sleeve too. He had a man in his troop, possibly a deserter, who could play the bugle. When Kit's bugler sounded a call, which communicated with distant troops, Satanta would cause confusion by sounding another call. Although no great harm was done, serious mischief was possible because the men behind the walls were almost overrun by the various Indian attacks. What saved the day were the mountain howitzers. Kit had ordered Lieutenant George Pettis to set them up on a rise some distance away. The fire from these cannons held the Indian charges in check. Had Satanta's bugler confused Pettis, the day could have been lost.

As it was, by late in the afternoon, with ammunition running low, Kit realized he couldn't hold the position. Worse, To-hauson's warriors might discover and attack his supply train. He had to fall back to the baggage train, left thirty miles away. Should the Indians destroy the supply wagons, all could be lost. But could he withdraw from the shelter of the walls?

The Kiowa, seeing the whites trying to sneak away, ignited the tall grass in the river bottom. The flames cut off an escape route. The smoke from the fires was used to hide further Indian attacks. But Kit Carson was an old Indian fighter. He knew a few tricks too. He started his own fire in the shorter upland grasses. The smoke from this fire was used to cover his men when they fell back to the cannon. About nightfall, before completely disengaging, Kit ordered some soldiers to torch the village of 176 teepees close at hand. Up in smoke went the winter shelter for a thousand or more of the Kiowa and Kiowa-Apache. The Kiowa-Apache chief, Iron Shirt, for some reason refused to leave his teepee. He was killed by the flames and smoke inhalation. Also destroyed were the Indian's winter supplies, including innumerable buffalo robes.

In the dead of night, Kit's fighters rejoined the wagon train. They camped the night and began a withdrawal for New Mexico the next day. The Indians had had enough of the fight too. The army command retreated up the Canadian River valley without incident. Altogether, Kit lost six men with twenty-two more wounded. Indian casualties ranged between 100 and 150 killed. Millie Durgan was indeed rescued.

General Carleton was pleased with the results of this battle. Though not a knockout blow, Kit had achieved as much as practical, given the number of his troops and the vastly larger opposition. During a period when regular military forces were occupied elsewhere, he had shown that the U.S. forces could inflict damage on the enemies. This was Kit's last Indian fight. Although it may well have been the most intense and largest of his career, Kit himself seems to have not been all that impressed by his victory.

COLONEL CHIVINGTON
AND THE SAND CREEK MASSACRE

- 1864 -

THE EVENING OF NOVEMBER 28, 1864, FOUND upwards of eight hundred mounted soldiers trotting their horses across the prairie northeast of Fort Lyon, Colorado. Marching in columns four abreast, they were heading for Sand Creek and the village of Black Kettle, One Eye, White Antelope, and Left Hand. At their head rode Colonel John Chivington.

Colonel Chivington was a huge man, weighing almost three hundred pounds. Before the Civil War broke out, he had made a living as a Methodist minister. But the war showed he had a talent for military service, as he forsook his first career as a preacher of peace and became a local legend as a fighting man. When the Confederates under Colonel Henry Sibley advanced north from El Paso along the Rio Grande, Chivington proved to be the man of the hour. The rebels marched north into New Mexico, capturing Albuquerque and Santa Fe. Union forces from Colorado met them at Glorieta Pass. The main fight between the Northern and Southern forces ended in a draw. But Chivington, leading a detachment of volunteers, came upon the Confederates' supply train. He attacked the lightly defended wagons, drove their defenders from the field, and then destroyed the supplies. Without ammunition and provisions the rebels had no choice but to fall back to Texas. This action had made Chivington a hero in Colorado. And now Chivington was certain the action his men were about to engage in would make him famous from one end of America to the other. He was indeed correct, but not in the way he hoped.

Shortly after dawn on the morning of November 29, Chivington and Colonel George Shoup ascended a slight rise. Below them glistened the slender thread of ice-rimmed Sand Creek. To their left sprawled the hundred lodges of Black Kettle's village. The yapping of dogs and the hurried movement in the village indicated that the troops had been spotted. Chivington gave the order to attack to Shoup, commander of the Colorado Third Cavalry, which had been nicknamed the Bloodless Third.

The columns of soldiers poured out from behind the ridge in a classic pincer movement. Lieutenant Luther Wilson and three companies were detailed to separate the Indians' horse herd, some distance from camp, from the men rushing toward their war ponies. Succeeding in this move, Wilson then turned toward the village. Chivington ordered his men to remove their overcoats. Then shouting, "Remember the murdered women and children on the Platte," he commanded his men to dismount and commence shooting into the hapless village. A cannon fired over the heads of the cavalrymen into the mass of teepees.

Learning of the presence of soldiers, Black Kettle ran up the huge Stars and Stripes he'd obtained from President Lincoln on a visit to Washington in 1862. Below it hung a white flag. As men, women, and children scurried around him seeking shelter, he called out that there was no need to flee. The village would be protected by the American flag. The soldiers would see they were among friends. He stood by this belief even as bullets whizzed around him. His wife was struck by one bullet and then another. Only after many more shots poured into his teepee did he turn and run, helping his wife along. White Antelope, upon seeing the assault, ran out of his lodge holding his hands in the air and shouting at the troopers. This gesture of peace didn't work, so White Antelope waded into Sand Creek in front of the village. He crossed his arms over his chest. He stood there signifying to all that the village was peaceful and did not want to fight. The soldiers paid no heed. He was struck by a hail of bullets and fell into the bloody waters of the creek.

Meanwhile, some of the Cheyenne men managed to form in a battle line, drawing fire to themselves to give the noncombatants a chance to escape. They fired volley after volley of arrows. At short range, arrows could be quite effective, but, shooting at the dismounted cavalrymen in the distance, the warriors found their bows and arrows were practically useless. Then the cannon was trained on their battle line. The warriors broke and ran. Many of the Indians ran up the creek where a few cottonwood and willow trees, along with the low hills bordering the creek, provided some cover. Farther on, the hills formed unscalable bluffs. Further passage was blocked. Those that made it to this point began digging in the sandy bottom, scrambling to provide some protection from the bullets whizzing about. Most were women and children, but the men among them fired back at the soldiers, preventing, for the time being, an all-out assault.

In the meantime, a soldier who found himself in the Indian village called to Colonel Chivington. He said he and others were trapped. The colonel told him to come out and bring the others. One of those was Blackfoot John Smith, who was married to a Cheyenne woman and traded and lived with the Cheyenne. Smith crossed to the bluecoat lines and followed along, sometimes running, sometimes walking, as the soldiers pushed up the creek to where the Cheyenne made their last stand. He saw the bodies of five or six soldiers killed by the warriors below the bluffs.

When the firing ceased in midafternoon, about a hundred corpses lay huddled near the bluffs. Approximately thirty were warriors. Seventy women and children were also killed. Altogether hundreds of Indians died, mostly women and children, and just a handful of troopers fell, some evidently from friendly fire. And the atrocities were not over. Troopers waded among the Indians, scalping, searching for souvenirs, sometimes committing gruesome acts such as mutilating the bodies of the dead enemy. The son of Blackfoot John Smith, Jack Smith, was told by troopers that he was worse than any Indian. Jack, heartsick at the carnage and the death of many of his friends, said to go ahead and kill him. A cowardly soldier cut a hole in the wall of the teepee in which Jack was lodged. He poked his pistol through and shot Jack in the side. Other old-time mountain men and Cheyenne traders were almost killed by the arrogant soldiers as well.

How could such things occur? Two months previously the very chiefs who were gunned down had discussed peace with the governor of the territory of Colorado in Denver. They had been conducted to that city by Major Edward Wynkoop of Fort Lyon. At first Governor John Evans refused Major Wynkoop's request to talk to them. After several days the governor relented and heard their side of the story.

While admitting some responsibility, the chiefs said most of the Indian attacks during the summer were caused by other bands, especially the Kiowa and Comanche. Also wreaking havoc were the Yankton Sioux from Minnesota. These Sioux had rebelled in the early days of the Civil War, killing seven hundred whites. They had been driven from that state and were now causing depredations on the plains. Black Kettle offered his young men as auxiliary soldiers to help the bluecoats drive these enemies from the plains. Finally, Governor Evans and even Colonel Chivington seemed satisfied with the chiefs. They told them to return to their people and to do as Major Wynkoop commanded and all would be well.

Neither the chief nor Wynkoop understood two things. The first was that Governor Evans owed his loyalty to the new settlers of Colorado. These folks greatly outnumbered the old-timers like William Bent and Blackfoot John Smith. The old-time Americans lived among and made their living by trading with the Indians. The new settlers had first been attracted to Colorado just six years earlier in 1858. A gold strike lured them to the territory. These people saw the Indians as threats. As long as Indians roamed the plains and mountain valleys, they believed, whites couldn't mine, ranch, or farm without fear of a sudden Indian attack. They were determined to drive all Indians from the area.

Their second reason for not wanting to have peace talks had to do with the Colorado Third Volunteers. Governor Evans had lobbied hard to get funds for this force. The money made available would support the force for just one hundred days. If it was shown that Indians wanted to sue for peace, Governor Evans would look foolish.

Black Kettle and the other chiefs returned to the plains of eastern Colorado. Major Wynkoop told them to camp on Sand Creek. Then on November 5, Wynkoop received orders from his commander in Kansas. He was to report to Fort Riley and turn command over to Major Scott Anthony. Wynkoop was devastated. So were the officers in his command. A letter was penned supporting Wynkoop's policies and signed by all officers at the post. On November 26 Major Wynkoop boarded the mail stage for Kansas. Two days later Chivington's Third Cavalry marched into the post. Their orders would expire in less than a month. Chivington might not know where any true hostiles were, but he knew that the scouts at Fort

Lyon were aware of the location of Black Kettle's band. On the way he put William Bent and others he thought might warn Black Kettle under guard. That evening the troopers marched to Black Kettle's village, and the "battle" commenced at dawn.

Chivington thought he would be hailed as a hero for his activities at Sand Creek. He hoped to parlay his reputation as Indian fighter into high political office. The first battle reports, supplied by Chivington himself, cast him in a favorable light. But bit by bit the truth began to creep abroad. Congress called for an investigation. Major Wynkoop was sent back to Fort Lyon to ferret out the facts. Chivington escaped official censure, but forever after his name was mud.

Kit Carson left an eloquent assessment of Chivington's actions: "To think of that dog Chivington up thar at Sand Creek! Whoever heerd of sich doings among Christians! Them pore Injuns had our flag flyin' over 'em. Well here come that durn Chivington and his cusses. They'd bin out huntin' hostile Injuns, and couldn't find none. So they just pitched into these friendlies and massa-creed them in cold blood. And ye call these civilized men Christians and the Injuns savages, du ye? 'Tain't natural for brave men to kill women and little children."

Black Kettle survived the Sand Creek Massacre. So did his wife, even though her body was pierced by nine balls. Black Kettle continued to advocate peace with the whites. His reason, no doubt, was pragmatic—he did not think the Cheyenne could survive unless they cooperated with the whites. Ironically, both Black Kettle and his wife were killed in another massacre a few years later during the so-called Battle of the Washita in present-day Oklahoma. The instigator of that atrocity was George Custer. Unlike Chivington he was praised for what was in actuality another low point in the annals of the American military. However, also, unlike Chivington, he was repaid in kind by the Indians, notably the Northern Cheyenne and Sioux, at the Little Bighorn.

FRANZ HUNING'S LOST TRAIN

- 1866 -

FOR THIRTEEN YEARS FRANZ HUNING HAD TRAVELED the Santa Fe Trail. He started out as a lowly bull whacker and worked up to merchant prince. He could speak English, German, and Spanish. He had a passable knowledge of French and Italian. He now owned a store in Albuquerque and traveled back and forth along the trail freighting his own goods. He had been warned at the end of the railroad, Junction City, Kansas, to hold up a few days. Others were readying their wagons to roll for the Southwest en masse because the Cheyenne Dog Soldiers and their allies were on the warpath.

However, rather than wait for others to form an impregnable moving fortress, Franz set out alone. His plug train was made up of seven wagons, a carriage, and an ambulance. In the ambulance rode his mother-in-law and her sixteen-year-old son. He made his way south thirty miles to Lost Springs, where he got on the Old Santa Fe Trail. His wagons made their way west about forty-five miles. At the Little Arkansas crossing, he began having second thoughts about pushing on with such a small company. He asked Captain Edward Byrne of the Tenth Cavalry stationed there for a troop escort. The captain refused him. His troops were deployed in a different manner, taking the laundresses on a picnic. By now, suspecting the worst, Franz rode ahead of the train, a keen eye peeled for any sign of hostiles.

But he was looking in the wrong place. The teamsters at the end of the train raised the alarm, hollering, "Indians, Indians!" At first he could not see them on account of a dense growth of sunflowers along the road. The wily braves, Kiowa, Arapaho, and Cheyenne, had sneaked up on foot, and they made no noise in the weeds and soft sandy soil. Franz jumped off his own saddle mule and ran to the third wagon from the front. He leveled his Spencer carbine at the lead Indian. But it was too late. His shot missed and the Indians succeeded in stampeding the mules pulling four wagons, the carriage, and the ambulance with the woman and her son. The vehicles lurched to a halt in deep sand two hundred yards off the trail, and the warriors set about their grim work. But Franz was hardly in a position to idly watch all this.

Ten Indians on horses, accompanied by a horde of warriors afoot, seeing their chance now turned their attention to the three remaining wagons. Franz sighted down the barrel of his rifle, and with a click, the hammer dropped but no shot fired. His gun had jammed! In the meantime his saddle mule stampeded off with the loose stock. Franz scrambled to keep up with the remaining wagons. If the mules pulling the wagons joined in the stampede, they would all be lost.

But the drivers, who rode the first mule ahead of the left front wheel, kept the animals in rein. Ultimately the remaining wagons were run together into a corral. Given the small numbers of those inside the circled wagons, they wouldn't have stood a chance against a concerted Indian attack. But the Indians had a better way to torture Franz Huning. They lashed the goods he had recently paid hard cash for onto the backs of his mules. Things too large to pack, such as kegs of whiskey, were stove in and set afire. But that was nothing compared to the other event going on. In the distance he witnessed a huge crowd of warriors gathering. They were laughing and whooping with joy. He knew those braves were having their way with his mother-in-law, as that was the practice of prairie Indians. The pistol shot, when it came, was a relief. The poor woman would not have to live with indignity in her fading years. Later teamsters told him his brother-in-law had been killed almost immediately.

At this point Franz saddled a mule and flew to Fort Zarah, just east of present-day Great Bend, Kansas. No soldiers were at hand, but two civilian scouts set out in an ambulance "as fast as [their] mules could take them, hitting only the high places." The two scouts were "armed to the teeth and spoiling for a fight" according to the memoirs of one of them, Captain Charles Christy. His partner "Roma was one of the bravest fighters I ever saw," Christy reported. Roma "had no fear of anything living and fighting Indians was the breath in his nostrils." They found under Huning's carriage the naked body of the driver, scalped and mutilated. In the ticking of a featherbed, two more bodies were discovered, so badly disfigured that the scouts thought they were both women, although they were Franz's mother-in-law and brother-in-law.

Christy and Roma unceremoniously heaped the bodies into the ambulance. They covered about a mile on the return trip to the fort when "there came suddenly streaming from a distant copse on our right a body of mounted Indians. They rode galloping toward us, firing and yelling as they came. [Roma] faced the rear and sat astride the bodies in the bottom of the ambulance. He fired at the Indians, keeping the bullets flying from his carbine as fast as he could. As for the mules, they were doing their part nobly. They leaned well in their collars and settled down to a pace that made their legs look like fringe, while they flew along like birds. With the help of Roma's gun we held our distance in advance of the yelling horde for four miles. By that time we saw the dust raised by the soldiers, who were approaching on the double-quick. Then with a parting yell and volley, the Indians turned and rode away and we saw no more of them."

Franz returned to his wife, Ernestine, in Albuquerque. In time the mental scars of the events on the prairie healed. Together they produced a distinguished family of merchants and, especially, writers. Franz built a large house called locally Huning Castle. Until 1955, when it was torn down, the mansion was one of the most pointed-out landmarks in Albuquerque. By then the family home lay on another notable American trail, Route 66.

THE BATTLE AT FOSSIL CREEK STATION

- 1869 -

WHEN CHARLEY SYLVESTER HOLLERED, "INDIANS," Johnny Roenigk thought he was just having a little fun. Charley was the work gang's comedian, prone to making jokes.

At twenty-one Johnny was the youngest of the seven men maintaining the tracks on the Union Pacific Railroad, Eastern Division, out of Fossil Creek Station, some 250 miles west of Kansas City. He was also the most cautious. Frequently, when passing the gun rack in the morning, he would pick up an extra rifle. Many of the men did not care to go to the trouble of carrying a weapon. Besides, the Indians never attacked. Although just barely twenty-one, Johnny had worked the longest of his work party on the railroad. He had passed the graves, one about every mile, of those killed by Indians while building the roadbed. And not far from where the men were working lay a grave of a man killed two years earlier. All this, along with a generally cautious disposition, made him particularly wary.

Earlier he had seen something that resembled a bay pony at a distance of about a mile. Everyone in the work party thought he had just seen an antelope made huge by the flickering plains sunlight. The brilliant light often made things look larger than they were. The stories of ravens mistaken on the prairie for buffalo were legion. And the flat Kansas plain was so level it was impossible to be taken unaware—in most instances. But the men were working in an area where an arm of a prairie river with deep rugged canyons approached to within a quarter mile of the tracks. The Cheyenne were familiar with the geography, having ambushed the track workers two years before. Johnny watched, astonished and appalled, as Indians on horseback poured out of the ravine. "Yes, they are Indians," another said, confirming Johnny's observation.

The Indians charged, "screaming like demons."

Johnny grabbed his Spencer carbine and bag of ammo and began stuffing shells into the stock, loading it. The Spencer was the first successful repeating rifle. Earlier repeaters did not pack the wallop of the Civil War–era musket. But the Spencer's .52 caliber bullet was big enough and its muzzle velocity powerful enough to compare favorably with those firearms. One hundred thousand of them had been put into service by Union forces during the Civil War. In Johnny's excitement, he crammed eight shells into magazine. It only held seven shots.

The gun jammed.

Johnny fumbled with the stock and extracted the extra shell. He shouldered the weapon and fired. The Indians bore down. Their bullets were kicking up dust all around. In the meantime the other six men crowded aboard the handcar and screamed at Johnny to jump on. Turning to look, he saw the car was under way, and the rest of the crew was already thirty yards down the track toward the station. He had to jump on the car while running, Indian bullets whizzing around him.

The Indians seemed just as excited as the men on the handcar.

Their shots were going wild. Johnny later remarked that he had seen a lot of poor marksmanship in his time, but the Indians' firing was the worst he'd ever witnessed, thankfully.

The men on the handcar knew they could outrun horses. They had done exactly that a few months earlier. A group of horsemen appeared and the section gang jumped on the handcar. The track went around a curve. The horsemen took a straight-line shortcut, but the handcar outpaced them easily. Later, the horsemen trotted up to the station with a white flag. They were buffalo soldiers of the Tenth Cavalry out of Fort Hays, who the railroad men had mistaken for Indians.

And now the handcar was outdistancing the Indians too.

Then another bunch of Indians broke from cover—ahead of the handcar. The men were surrounded, with only three of them carrying weapons. They quit pumping the handcar and picked up their Spencers, and the speed slacked off. Johnny fired and hit nothing. Indians' guns were going off all over the place. Bullets were whizzing by. Figuring it was impossible to reach the station, Johnny, upon seeing a depression ahead, called, "Let's go in the culvert." Someone grunted no, and on they went.

The Indians' main danger seemed to be each other. They were galloping along on both sides of the tracks in front and back. Realizing this, they opened up in front, partly from the effect of the Spencers and partly from fear of hitting their comrades. Already the handcar had made a half mile. It was only a mile to the station.

Maybe they would make it.

But the Indians, seeing that the car was speeding up, pressed close, never minding the tempting targets they made. Johnny and the other men raised their guns. Trying to aim true was tough. The small handcar had seven desperate men on it. Four were pumping the levers that pushed the car on while three were trying to fire. The Indians, seeing the rifles leveled, would slide off the backs of their horses and cling to the side, completely out of sight. Now many of the Indians were out of bullets. They'd fire arrows from the notch between the horse's muzzle and throat so the arrows shot over the handcar.

The crew meanwhile gained hope. They were halfway back to the station. Amazing as it might seem, no one had been injured.

Then one of the men on the handcar was hit. It was impossible for the injured man to hang on to the car, crowded with frantically gesturing men, tearing down the tracks. No one thought—or dared—to take time out to grab the wounded man. He tumbled off. Indians jumped from their ponies, surrounding the man. Then another called, "Oh, God." Johnny turned to look at him and then went back to firing at the attackers. That fellow too slipped off the car, and Indians leapt to the ground around him. One of the two men was Alexander McKeefer, a giant of a man, more than six feet tall and broad of chest. Just moments before he'd been in the prime of life.

Johnny blasted at those around the fallen men. He hadn't the time to check his effectiveness. A shower of arrows clattered against the handcar. Blood covered the surfaces. With a thunk, an arrow got George Seeley in the thigh. He pulled it out, cocked his Spencer, and fired again. Johnny noticed only he and another man had not been hit.

Now the station, which was just a couple of sunken cabins called dugouts and a water tank, was in sight, a quarter mile away. Modest as its fortifications were, the Indians seemed to be intimidated by them. They began falling back.

Then the last three shots were fired. Johnny felt a pinch in his chest, like a wasp sting. Spurts of blood gushed from his mouth and nose.

John Cook, the builder of the large dugout, met the men, rifle in hand. He ushered them inside and prepared for an attack. The ammunition was laid out, as were most of the defenders. Of the five survivors from the handcar, four were wounded. All three sprawled out on blankets on the floor. Johnny checked his wound. It was a hole square in the center of his chest. He figured he was a goner. He said his prayers and watched the clock ticking on the wall. Every time the minute hand advanced, he supposed that meant he had just one minute less to live.

Only John Cook and one other were unwounded. They took turns as lookout on the roof. Today, Cook's dugout cabin would be called earth sheltered. The roof was constructed of railroad ties, on top of which soil was mounded for insulation. Since most of the structure was underground, from a distance it looked like a small rise in the prairie. The men on the roof, keeping watch, appeared like prairie dogs peeping out of their hole. All afternoon Indians circled at a distance. To the east they could be seen tearing up track. Then as dark approached, a large mass was observed in the south, moving in their direction. No, it wasn't more Indians. Thankfully, it was a herd of buffalo.

The Indians surrounded the herd, killing five buffalo using lances or arrows. Then after butchering the animals, they proceeded off to the northeast. A few minor injuries occurred at midnight when the approaching westbound train overturned. Then the skirmish at Fossil Creek was history.

Though shot straight through the chest, Johnny, after months of recuperation, completely recovered from his wound. For a time the railroad provided an easy job for him in the safer area around Manhattan. By the following spring he was ready to resume life on the frontier. When he boarded the train for the open prairie, he went prepared. He took along one thousand rounds of Spencer ammunition.

LUCIEN MAXWELL,
MOUNTAIN MAN MILLIONAIRE

- 1870 -

On July 6, 1870, the mountain man Lucien Maxwell found himself surrounded by wood. The wood was not the woods of the Rocky Mountains where he had spent his early days. Rather it was the luxuriantly paneled boardroom of a law firm on Williams Street in New York City. Maxwell was handed a pen. A dotted line was indicated. He signed on the line. Another witnessed the document. With these two signatures, Lucien's claim to hundreds of thousands of acres in northern New Mexico and southern Colorado were transferred from the mountain man to a corporation owned by Europeans.

Was this son of mixed Irish and French-Canadian parentage taken advantage of by wily easterners and Englishmen? The answer can be given in two words: not hardly.

Lucien was born in 1820 in Kaskaskia, Illinois. Kaskaskia, though in Illinois, was a sort of failed Saint Louis. Many a western adventurer started off or returned there. One of those was Lucien's grandfather, Pierre Menard. Originally from Quebec, Menard had ranged through the mountains of the West as one of the first generation of mountain men. But he returned to Illinois and Missouri, married, opened a store, and ultimately became the first lieutenant governor of Illinois. The Maxwell side of the family emigrated from Ireland. A priest uncle had been sent to Missouri to minister to the small French colony there when the territory still belonged to Spain and France. That uncle received a land grant as part of his pay. After the United States bought the Louisiana Purchase, his claims were subject to intense legal scrutiny, but they were ultimately upheld. Finally, Lucien, unlike many mountain men, received two years of schooling. All of these elements, his schooling, and the experience of his relatives' realizing a profit from a grant of land, helped Lucien recognize the immense value of western real estate.

But at the ripe age of seventeen, Lucien was happy to get out of school and travel the Santa Fe Trail to Bent's Old Fort in southeastern Colorado. There he met Kit Carson, who was twenty-six. The two would be lifelong associates and friends. At the time Kit, originally from central Missouri, had been in the West for ten years. He'd married an Arapaho woman, Singing Grass, and he was already locally famous for his exploits in the mountains. Lucien may have gone trapping with Kit. In any case he spent years in the mountains of Colorado, Utah, Wyoming, and New Mexico and adjacent areas. He lived with bands of Indians and fought against other Indians with them. He attended one or more of the annual rendezvous of the trappers, including probably the last one in 1840. Two years later, back in Missouri on a steamboat, he and his friend Kit Carson met the man who made Kit Carson's name a household word.

That man was John C. Fremont, an army officer sent to "explore" the West, an area already very well known by the likes of Lucien, Kit, and other mountain men. The report of Fremont's expedition was published by the government. Widely read, that report brought the feasibility of vehicles crossing the Rockies to the attention of eastern Americans. Shortly, thereafter, wagons began heading over the prairie to South Pass in Wyoming, the designated pass through the mountains, and the Oregon Trail was born. Published accounts of later expeditions made Kit Carson's name a household word. Lucien, who was along on most of Fremont and Kit's exploits, was also accorded praise in the accounts. Once when Fremont, Lucien, and several others were besieged by Arapahos, Lucien called out to the attacking warriors, "Don't you know me?" The braves recognized Lucien. The battle abruptly ceased, and the two parties camped together, sharing roast buffalo for dinner.

Events of much more importance to Lucien, and probably Kit too, happened in Taos, New Mexico. At the time Taos was the New Mexican headquarters for American mountain men. One of the very first of these "Americans" was Charles Beaubien. Though born in Quebec and ordained as a Catholic priest, Beaubien forsook his roots. He migrated to Saint Louis, working for a time in the enterprises of the Chouteaus. Upon the opening of the Santa Fe Trail, Beaubien was among the first foreigners to travel down it with the intention of trying his hand at a life in New Mexico. He took out citizenship papers, changed his given name to Carlos, married sixteen-year-old Pabla Lobato, and, in time, grew wealthy, at least by local standards.

Lucien struck up a friendship with Carlos, and he married his daughter, Luz. As an adult woman Luz was described as being a great beauty with hazel eyes and dark hair. At the time of her wedding to Lucien, however, she was only in her early teens. Kit Carson, after the death of his wife and a later divorce, also married a Taos woman, Josefa Jaramillo. Leaving their wives at home in Taos, the two young men pursued the lives of trappers and guides in the mountains and on the plains. While Lucien was doing this, his father-in-law, Don

Carlos, was preparing the foundation for the family empire. The Mexican government believed settlement of the territory along the boundary with the United States was necessary to keep the Americans from ultimately claiming those lands. Since the Spanish had not populated the area in their two-hundred-year occupation, they turned to foreigners to help them. Carlos Beaubien in association with local secretary of state Pablo Miranda filed for a grant east of the Rockies in northwestern New Mexico. The property came to about two million acres in New Mexico and adjoining sections of southern Colorado. This grant was immediately approved by Governor Manuel Armijo. Seeing an opportunity, Don Carlos applied for another grant, this time in the name of his sixteen-year-old son. It was for about a million acres, and that grant too met with approval.

Almost all land grants, from any government at any time, came with conditions. The chief condition almost always was settlement. Unless settlers, preferably married couples with children, occupied the grant and commenced economic activity, grants became null and void. The granting agencies wanted citizens occupying the land who would become taxpaying supporters of the local government. Don Carlos was woefully unprepared to meet these conditions. Local folks, led by the Catholic pastor Father Jose Antonio Martinez, were hostile to his claims. They would not agree to the legitimacy of the grant by helping him settle it. And in the 1840s New Mexico was far too distant from the United States and offered too few incentives to tempt American settlers.

Beaubien was saved by history. First, Texans invaded. Their expedition was easily defeated. But land pirates, encouraged by the Texans, continued operating for several years. Moving into the unprotected plains east of the Rockies was unfeasible, so the Mexican government didn't rescind the grant. Then the Mexican-American War broke out. The United States occupied New Mexico. Beaubien's concerns now were to have the new American administration certify his claims to the land. Getting them to do that would not be easy. The Mexican law forbade grants larger than eleven miles square. Both of Don Carlos's were much larger.

After the Treaty of Hidalgo ended the Mexican-American War, Lucien crossed the Sangre de Cristo Mountains to Rayado Creek, his father-in-law urging him to begin settlement of their vast estate. He erected a log cabin, but he planned to build a regular house with real planed lumber. The new wing would have the look of fancy urban houses. Supplies for this ambitious project were required, and Lucien went to Missouri to get them. On his return Jicarilla Apaches attacked him. Seven thousand dollars of goods and cash were lost. Even worse, a bullet struck Lucien in the neck. Fortunately, his friend, known as Indian George, nursed him. Another friend, Dick Wootton, learning of Lucien's scrape from friendly Indians, lit out with a relief force. Lucien spent the winter recovering from his wound. The next spring found Lucien, accompanied by Kit Carson, back on Rayado Creek.

This time the houses he and Kit built used the local building material of choice, adobe. Lucien's house, added to over the years, grew to twenty rooms and was set inside an adobe-walled enclosure. Kit's was more modest. The Santa Fe Trail passed by the village. The small community of twenty or so families sold the produce they raised to passing traders. Kit was Indian agent and bought much of the provisions for the Indians. Fort Union, only forty miles away, took in the rest of the valley's produce. Lucien's community prospered. But Lucien wasn't necessarily happy staying in one place. Once, Lucien, Kit, and Dick Wootton drove a herd of thousands of sheep north to Wyoming. There they turned west and headed across the northern deserts and plains to California. Gold miners needed meat, and they were willing to pay top dollar. It is claimed Wootton pocketed $42,000 (about $700,000 today), and Kit and Lucien made similar sums. Thanks to this prosperity, Lucien gave a standing invitation to one and all to stop by his house. Dinner, served at noon, might find any number of Mexicans, Indians, and American traders all sitting down at his table. Some of those invited knew Lucien so vaguely that they offered to pay for their food.

But with all this prosperity, Lucien still had to face one burning question. Would American courts recognize the grant from the New Mexican government? Now Lucien's family background with its experience with land grants began to pay off. Clearly, many thought the land grants were simply worthless paper. Pablo Miranda, who claimed joint ownership of the original grant, had so little faith in its worth that he offered to sell out for $2,500. Lucien agreed to this sum and paid the legal fees to boot. In other words, for $2,750 he obtained a claim to one million acres. For $500 he bought a one-sixth claim to Carlos's other grant of a million acres, and as the years wore on, he bought out the other heirs' claims for sums of about $3,500 each.

But what to do with all that property? People were moving onto it and staking claims. Although Lucien collected rents from some, many he allowed to homestead unmolested. After all he had scratched a living out of the soil himself. He knew how hard the pioneering life was. But he grew tired of managing so much land, and so Lucien eagerly snatched at a plan to sell his claim to the government for a Ute Indian reservation. But that prospect fell through, and then in 1869 the English company made its offer. Lucien knew the time had come. By now he and his wife, Luz, were the only owners of both of Carlos Beaubien's land claims. He traveled to New York, sold his claim, and collected his money. The sale of his huge residential complex and other land grants brought his cash payments to almost a million dollars, in a time when a million dollars was truly a fortune.

He returned to New Mexico and moved two hundred miles south to Fort Sumner, where he built an elegant house, played poker, raced quarter horses, and tried to turn a blind eye to the upshot of the sale. Almost immediately the company that bought his land claims began evicting those it considered squatters on its land. Given the experience of his uncle long ago back in Missouri, Lucien must have suspected something of the sort would happen. Perhaps that was why he moved two hundred miles away. In the resulting range war, known as the Colfax County War, dozens were killed, and the struggle continued until 1887. That was when the U.S. Supreme Court upheld the legality of both grants. The company had the legal right. There was no point fighting it. But by then Lucien was long gone, having died a mere five years after the sale of his immense tract of land. Luz, however, lived at least a quarter of a century more, dying in 1900 or perhaps 1907; as often happened in times gone by, accounts vary. Today, a huge Boy Scout camp occupies the site of Lucien's first cabin on the Rayado.

BAT AND THE TENDERFOOT

- 1874 -

IN THE SPRING OF 1874, A SIGHT APPEARED ON the streets of Dodge City that made the most jaded denizen of that notorious western city stop and take a gander. They were gawking at an Eastern dude who had just arrived in town. After renting a horse at the livery stable, he ran the animal up and down the streets of Dodge as though he owned the town. But as much as his actions, his getup caught everyone's attention. He wore a suit of black broadcloth that would have not been out of place in the business district of an eastern city. On his head rode a plug hat, and though stylish in New York City, it looked ridiculous under the blazing western sun. His vest was described as "a flowerbed," and his necktie was so colorful it rivaled a Rocky Mountain sunset. In Dodge City an outfit like that provoked much talk and laughter.

The man's name was John Fairchild. He came from Illinois. He had money. He had education. He even had a profession, that of lawyer. But what he wanted to be was a buffalo hunter. There was something rather winning in his way, and so, perhaps against their better judgment, a group of buffalo hunters agreed to let him join their band. On the day of departure, he showed up in a completely different getup. This time he was wearing a jacket and trousers of brown duck. He had on high-heeled stirrup boots with spurs that looked as big as wagon wheels, and his white cowboy hat could have been mistaken for an umbrella. A kerchief more brilliant than a Cheyenne pony painted for the warpath circled his neck while his belt bristled with a six-shooter, cartridges, and a butcher knife. They were "murderous looking weapons." He carried a .50-caliber buffalo rifle for which he'd paid $85, almost three months' salary for a freighter on the Santa Fe Trail at the time.

The company of hunters had not gotten far out onto the Cimarron Desert when they realized they had a problem with Fairchild. He had purchased that savage-looking butcher knife with one view in mind. He expected to scalp an Indian with it. And he wanted to hasten the day when this foul deed could be accomplished by attacking the first group of Indians encountered.

Talk like this was very disturbing. Experienced hunters knew they did not have to go looking for danger on the plains. It would come find them soon enough. They were traveling in country claimed by the Kiowa and the Comanche, considered the best irregular light cavalry in the world. For sure they didn't want to tempt fate by any rash actions of the sort Fairchild desired. The company decided something had to be done to set Fairchild straight, and the person detailed to come up with a suitable "experience" was the youngest among them, twenty-year-old Bartholomew Masterson.

Bartholomew had been born in Quebec, but as a youth he moved many times. While he was still a tyke, his father transferred the family to New York, then to Illinois, and finally to a farm near Wichita, Kansas. At this point Bartholomew had officially changed his name to William Barclay. But everyone knew him as Bat. Though still in his teens, he migrated to the buffalo range in western Kansas and spent a winter hunting buffalo. Bat was chosen as prankster in part because he was the youngest among the party. But perhaps more importantly Bat was also known to love playing practical jokes, and he was eager to carry out his mission.

Not far from camp stood a grove of trees. Hundreds of turkeys roosted in those trees each night. Bat asked Fairchild to go for a turkey hunt. First, they would wait until dark when the turkeys settled in. Then they would shoot them, aiming at their outlines against the sky. Unknown to Fairchild, three men, including Bat, had sneaked into the grove and started a fire at a location Bat had carefully chosen. Fairchild was so excited at the prospect of a hunt that the men had a difficult time keeping him in camp until the fire starters returned. Then, shortly after building a roaring fire, Bat sneaked back into camp. He and another man led Fairchild to the grove of trees.

The small group came around a bend in the creek and into a dense stand of timber. They stepped out from behind a large cottonwood to see the dim glow of the fire. Immediately, they slunk behind the large cottonwood and put their heads together. Bat told the others that the fire was an Indian fire. They had stumbled on an Indian camp. He added that he'd dreamed of Indians the last couple of nights. Then Bat's accomplice told Bat that he was mistaken—and just outright yellow. Besides, he said, Fairchild, by himself, could whip every Indian within fifty miles.

Just then a half dozen shots were fired by a man secreted in the woods. Bang, bang, bang. The bullets whipped through the trees overhead. Twigs and leaves floated down. The man who just a moment before had called Bat yellow started screaming. He ran for camp hollering bloody murder. Fairchild streaked hell-bent for leather right behind him. Bat brought up the rear, screaming and firing his six-shooter. Bat gradually dropped behind, keeping up the pretense that a terrible battle was going on. "Run, Fairchild. Run for your life," Bat hollered.

Fairchild shot past the first man. Bat had led him far enough away from camp that when he arrived, he was completely winded. Fairchild plopped face down on the ground, his eyes protruding from his head, his teeth clattering. The hunters circled round him. "What happened?" they wanted to know. For several minutes Fairchild gasped for air, trying to speak but failing. Finally, he croaked out one word: "Injuns."

What had happened to Bat and the other man, he was asked.

"Killed, I guess," Fairchild said.

"Are you sure they were Indians?" he was asked.

He said there were dozens, maybe hundreds, and he was sure they were Indians because he heard an arrow buzz past his head.

"Oh, men, he must be shot," one of the hunters proclaimed. The man grabbed a butcher knife and stuck the point under his collar. He slit Fairchild's shirt down his back and ripped it off. Another poured the contents of the coffeepot on him. All this made Fairchild think he had been wounded.

Then into camp bounded Bat and the other man. They rushed up to Fairchild and promptly upbraided him for abandoning them to their fate. But there was no time to bewail the issue. Serious business was at hand. There were hundreds of Indians camped in the patch of woods yonder. What should they do?

The men became involved in heated discussion. Some said the only thing to do was hitch up and head for Dodge immediately. The Indians wouldn't be able to follow their trail at night, they claimed. By daylight they'd be out of harm's way. Fairchild firmly backed this plan. Others said they were buffalo hunters and perfectly capable of holding their own. After much disagreement back and forth, the latter side appeared to win the argument. It was decided men would be posted around the camp.

Fairchild was given a spot on a high riverbank. The men told him it was important that he keep a sharp look out. Otherwise the Indians might attack his position and wipe out everyone. In actuality his spot was almost perfectly defensible. The high bank he was on and the swift river flowing beneath it made a surprise attack from that point impossible. But he was scared out of his wits and he believed the men.

While he kept guard, the hunters snuggled into their bedrolls. Fairchild discovered he'd been made fun of in the morning. He was so mad the hunters were afraid he might try to shoot someone. He refused to eat breakfast and stalked off. For days he fumed, but after a while he came around. And no longer did he brag about scalping an Indian. Nor did the hunters have to worry about him starting a needless war.

While John Fairchild faded into history, Bat Masterson went on to become a legendary figure in the West. Beginning as buffalo hunter, gambler, and gunfighter, later he was sheriff of Ford County (Dodge City), Kansas. At Denver he managed prizefighters and wrote a sports column for a newspaper. At the turn of the century, he moved to New York, where he was promptly arrested for carrying a firearm. He became a noted sports writer, friend of President Teddy Roosevelt, and frequent guest at the White House. He died after the First World War. As for Fairchild what happened to him cannot be stated for certain. One old buffalo hunter said the last time he saw him, the former eastern lawyer was kneeling beside a carcass of the monarch of the plains. His shirtsleeves were rolled up, he had a half inch of tan on his face, and he was happily skinning the buffalo that he had shot.

THE "UNCLE DICK" CHUFFS INTO
SANTA FE, ALMOST

- 1880 -

THE RAP ON THE DOOR CAME AT ABOUT TEN O'CLOCK. Richens Wootton, widely known as Uncle Dick, was turning in for the night. His
house, on a lonesome stretch of the mountain route of the Santa Fe
Trail, lay far up Raton Pass at an elevation of more than seven thousand feet. Way back at the end of the Civil War, Uncle Dick had
improved twenty-seven miles of the roughest section of the trail. He
bridged streams, and he blasted cuts on the high grades and filled low
spots. Then he installed a tollgate and collected a modest fee from all
who passed. But Uncle Dick had learned it wasn't always wise to
answer the door late at night.

Once before he had been summoned about bedtime. On that
occasion he'd heard a cry for help. Earlier in the evening, he had
seen four men in heated discussion. He reasoned that three of them
were doing violence to the fourth. He asked himself, "Should I ren-
der aid and possibly put myself at risk?" He decided to remain

safely indoors. In the morning he found a dead body on the doorstep. When the culprits were found—whom Dick identified—he learned that one had been stationed at his door with orders to shoot if Uncle Dick emerged.

That memory was powerful incentive to keep the portal barred. But the men at the door called to Uncle Dick, urging him to open. They said they were from the Atchison, Topeka, and Santa Fe Railroad. Their voices seemed eastern and educated. That wasn't enough to get Dick to swing open the door. What did they want with him, especially in the middle of the night?

They said the good people of Trinidad, Colorado, had tipped them off. The Denver and Rio Grande was about to start construction on a railroad through Uncle Dick's pass. The Santa Fe men said they wanted to make a deal.

Build through his pass? He hadn't been consulted about this. Uncle Dick knew the people of Trinidad were annoyed with the Denver and Rio Grande because it had tried to destroy their town. It put its station at the new town of El Moro, thinking townspeople would have to move and buy Denver and Rio Grande real estate. This caused much hard feeling toward the railroad. Despite past experience Uncle Dick unbolted the door and in burst the two Santa Fe men. They identified themselves as Albert Robinson and William Morley. It was apparent from their very first sentences that the railroad men had done their homework. They didn't treat Uncle Dick like a backwoods rube.

They seemed to know he was from good southern stock, his father being a Virginia planter. They seemed to understand, also, that Uncle Dick had wide experience in the West. As a young man of twenty in 1836, Dick had signed on with a Santa Fe–bound wagon train. Thereafter, he pursued the career of mountain man but by a strange turn of events had become the owner of this stretch of pass.

He, along with his best friends, Kit and Lucien, had trailed thousands of sheep to California during the gold rush and made a killing. Lucien, with plans to build the biggest mansion in the West, took his share of the proceeds to Kansas City. There he bought all the fixings and was headed into New Mexico over the mountains when the Jicarilla Apaches thought they'd get their share of the proceeds. Lucien was wounded and left for dead. He probably would have died had it not been for Uncle Dick. He got word of Lucien's plight and hotfooted it across the Sangre de Cristos to help Lucien.

Later out of friendship and perhaps a sense of gratitude, Lucien, who supposedly owned title to Raton Pass among more than three million acres, sold Uncle Dick the parcel of land around the pass. Uncle Dick, taking no chances on what many thought was a spurious land grant, asked for charters from the legislatures of the states his toll road ran through. Now fifteen years later, the Union Pacific had spanned the continent, and spur lines had extended down the front range of the Rockies to Denver. It was only natural that a railroad would follow the Santa Fe Trail into New Mexico. And it was also only natural that the Denver and Rio Grande would try to come through Raton Pass without asking Uncle Dick's blessing. He could see their argument. They'd claim he had the wagon toll concession from the states of Colorado and New Mexico. They were building a railroad, something not covered in Uncle Dick's charter. Their lawyers would take him to court, and he would not be able to afford to challenge them.

Uncle Dick liked the honest approach of the men who arrived in the dark. "The Santa Fe will do right by you," they promised.

"Well," Uncle Dick said, "I guess I'll have to get out of the way of the locomotive."

The men offered Uncle Dick $50,000.

Uncle Dick was coy. And the railroad men were impatient. They wanted to start work on the grading, immediately, in the dead of night. To help prevent cutthroat competition, the law read that once a railroad began building, no other could. The matter was extremely urgent. The telegraph lines of the Santa Fe and Denver and Rio Grande connected. Both sides sent coded messages, and both companies had broken the other's code. Robinson and Morley knew that the Denver and Rio Grande had decided to build through the pass. Worse, they had followed officials of the other line to a company hotel at El Moro at the bottom of the mountain where the D&RG's tracks ended. They might get a work gang out in the morning. So the Santa Fe had to begin construction this very night. Robinson and Morley agreed to pay Uncle Dick not less than the $50,000 if he would let them start tonight.

Uncle Dick not only agreed, but he offered to help the men himself, even though he was sixty-four years old. Robinson and Morley accepted his offer to work for them. They had brought a crew with them, and another Santa Fe agent, stationed on the New Mexico side, had camped high on the pass with another crew. All work gangs began grading operations—by lantern light. By morning, when the Denver and Rio Grande officials woke, they found the side of the mountain staked out for the Santa Fe tracks. The pass was the AT&SF's by right of prior construction.

It seemed only natural that the Atchison, Topeka, and Santa Fe Railroad would be the first to Santa Fe, right? Not necessarily. Like many early-day railroads, the name Atchison, Topeka, and Santa Fe was almost as long as the original rail line. When it finished its first installment in 1869—ten years after its founding—the AT&SF connected neither Santa Fe nor Atchison to Topeka. The rails ran only twenty-six miles south of Topeka, Kansas, to Burlingame, Kansas. But they did touch the Old Santa Fe Trail. As money was found to continue work, the AT&SF crept along the old trail, more or less. Railroads, though expensive to build, were much more efficient than wagon trains. But the AT&SF did not gather in the Santa Fe wagon trade because by this time the head of the trail was way out on the Colorado-Kansas border at end of the Kansas Pacific rail line. The AT&SF laid its rails in the Arkansas River valley for another reason—land.

The government wanted to enlarge its tax base and develop the state of Kansas. To do that, the government offered every other square mile of land within ten miles of the tracks to the railroad. Settlers needed the road to move the products they produced on the land. The railroad needed the money from the sale of the land to finance its push west. But there was a catch. In order to receive title to these lands, the AT&SF had to reach the Kansas-Colorado border by January 1, 1873. The railroad succeeded. These bottomlands were rich and could be irrigated from the river. The AT&SF's prosperity was assured, and the company built up the Arkansas River valley all the way to Pueblo, Colorado, thanks to the possibility of irrigation. It arrived in Pueblo in 1876. The next step across the Sangre de Cristo Mountains, and Raton Pass, would be expensive and risky. Should the railroad live up to its name and go to Santa Fe?

The financial data was not encouraging. Only $2 million worth of trade was freighted into Santa Fe the year previously. AT&SF's cars could haul that in a week. Would the railroad expend a fortune putting rails across the rugged mountain passes and then go broke? But the Denver and Rio Grande's actions spurred on the Santa Fe. It made the commitment to challenge Raton Pass, 7,990 feet high. And that brought them to Uncle Dick Wootton's doorstep.

The grade was too high for conventional engines. The AT&SF wired the Baldwin Locomotive Works in Pennsylvania to send the most powerful engine on earth. The locomotive was shipped west in pieces as it was too heavy to run over conventional railroads. Trestles would crunch under its immense weight. This monster engine was numbered 2403. Later, when construction of the road was complete, including a tunnel toward the top of the pass, the engine was rebuilt. No longer did the railroad need an engine powerful enough to lug tremendous loads on the temporary tracks over the top of the pass, but it was still used to power passenger and freight trains. And it retained its name, the "Uncle Dick," after Uncle Dick Wootton, whose cooperation allowed the AT&SF to truly become the Atchison, Topeka, and Santa Fe—well, almost.

The closest the AT&SF main line got to its namesake city, Santa Fe, was seventeen miles. Owing to the mountain blocking access from the east, a spur line was run from Lamy, New Mexico, into the capital city, and local trains transferred freight and passengers into Santa Fe. It is unlikely the powerful locomotive "The Uncle Dick" was employed for this minor run. But the railroad made the right choice in crossing into New Mexico. From the very first, despite their fears, the road turned a hearty profit.

Long after Santa Fe tracks crossed Raton Pass, railroad financiers resumed negotiations with Uncle Dick. If he didn't want $50,000, what did he want? Uncle Dick said, "You give me and my family a lifetime pass and $25 a month in groceries, and we'll call it square."

After Uncle Dick died in 1893, his wife got the pass and the $25 a month. After a while the Santa Fe doubled the payment, and then in 1930 they added another $25 a month.

When Mrs. Wootton died, an invalid daughter continued to receive assistance from the railroad. Uncle Dick said he built his toll road for old-age security. It worked out, for him and his family, better than he had planned.

PARKERVILLE, KANSAS, CELEBRATES THE FOURTH

- 1899 -

THE EVENING OF JULY 3, 1899, found the sheriff of Marion County, Kansas, galloping across the treeless Flint Hills of east central Kansas. A handful of deputies accompanied him, their faces stern. They were riding across the tallgrass prairie in order to break up a criminal enterprise. Although they didn't expect trouble, none could doubt the mastermind behind this conspiracy was an extremely brilliant and possibly dangerous man.

On entering the main street of the little town of Parkerville, a dozen miles from the county seat of Council Grove, they goaded their mounts. They flew by the train depot and the few shops on Main Street. They were headed for the village's only hotel, a two-story limestone building on the other side of the tracks. They went fast to keep anyone from tipping off the master criminal. Not far on the other side of the small park that had in more hopeful times been reserved for the county courthouse, they spotted the tall stone house.

Hastily running their mounts into the man's corral, the sheriff's men burst into the back door of the hotel. A frail old man dove for his shooting iron. The sheriff hollered for him to stop. "I got a warrant here, Charley Parker," he called to the first citizen and founder of the village. "You are to desist. We have knowledge that spiritous liquors and malted beverages are to be found on these premises." A quick search of the property turned up thirty-six cases of beer and sundry other spirits earmarked for an old-timey Fourth of July celebration the following day. The seventy-nine-year-old Parker was hauled in as a common bootlegger.

Charles Parker was no ordinary hotel keeper or bootlegger. Born in Connecticut in 1821, Parker was orphaned at the age of ten, after which he "pushed his own way through life." By the age of thirty, he was a teamster on the Santa Fe Trail. By the age of thirty-six, he had risen to the position of "conductor" or wagon master.

Once on the trail near present-day Dodge City, his train was confronted by two hundred Kiowa warriors. The Indians swarmed the roadway professing friendship. Being good friends, they pretended the freighters wouldn't mind their checking out the contents of the wagons. While some of the young men pressed under the canvas tilts, others casually armed their bows and sat on their horses looking ready for business as select goods were pitched to the ground. At this point Parker knew he'd been had. He called to the men to grab their weapons, shots were exchanged, and the band of Kiowa warriors slunk off. They trailed along behind, too far to shoot at but perfectly visible.

It was clear something needed to be done, and Chief Peshamo, understanding the situation, called on Parker. He congratulated the wagon boss for correctly handling the situation with the young raiders. At the same time the chief said the situation was tense. If some provisions were donated for the band's women and children, the chief said he thought the young men would behave themselves.

Parker ordered a hundred pounds of flour and crackers handed over. He also gave fifty pounds of coffee, sugar, and rice along with some butcher knives and tobacco. The plunder was taken and the Indians disappeared into the vastness of the plains. A few miles farther along, the warriors reappeared, this time in ambush, leaping out from a gully. The warriors shot two mules on a lead wagon, at which point the teamsters cut loose with their weapons. Later, Chief Peshamo bragged that this attack on the mules was part of a larger plan. He hoped to gain even more tribute from Parker.

Faced with difficulties like these, Parker turned for a time to innkeeping. His hotel was the most prominent establishment in Santa Fe, New Mexico, known as the Exchange at the time and the La Fonda for most of its long history. Located at the very end of the Santa Fe Trail, within a stone's throw of the city's plaza and the governor's palace, it was, according to old trail hand Captain Philip St. George Cooke, the oldest hostelry in the United States. Here Parker learned that the Indians were not the only creatures in the West that were wily. The local government harassed him for selling liquor to enlisted soldiers and for running a gaming establishment. Parker's biographer expressed great puzzlement as to how a man could get into trouble with the law for engaging in these pursuits. Such things had gone on at that address for hundreds of years

After the Civil War, Parker made his last eastward journey across the plains. Most people would have said the spot he chose to settle, twelve miles northwest of Council Grove, was smack on the American frontier. Raids by the Cheyenne and Sioux were still common fifty miles west, and the decimation of the vast herd of American bison had not yet begun. But to a grizzled old-timer, he was back in the States. Not for nothing had he spent decades in the transportation industry. The four hundred acres he acquired just happened to lie on the proposed route of the Missouri-Kansas-Texas (or KATY) Railroad. The train on its daily (then later three times a week) run stopped at his property. A town was laid out, naturally named Parkerville, and a thriving business district developed. An inn was needed for his community, and so those months managing the Exchange Hotel were put to good use. He built a two-story house with a front and rear staircase. He left out a hallway on the second floor. Hotel guests used the rooms in the front, and they were entertained by Charles (widely known as Charley) in a semiprivate taproom. In time a three-story steam-driven mill was added to his holdings. Up to 240 bushels of wheat a day could be ground into flour. When the supply of local wheat was exhausted, the mill sawed lumber from Parker's one-hundred-acre woodlot.

In 1871, at the age of fifty, the former teamster saw the opportunity to make his mark by attempting to capture the county seat from Council Grove. Both towns engaged in bare-knuckle electioneering. As election day approached, cattle drovers were enticed to the town and entertained lavishly. Likewise, craftsmen were engaged to erect or finish buildings of no immediate use. The results from the poll were disappointing to Parker. Morris County's population at that time was reckoned at 2,225, and 1,312 of them cast a vote. Almost nine hundred chose Council Grove with just over 30 percent going for Parkerville.

Though losing the county seat, the town continued to prosper. The business district added buildings, and houses kept on being built. The years passed. Charley's young wife ran away and died. He took another wife, this one closer to his age. By all appearances the new Mrs. Parker suited the old teamster just fine, and she liked him. By her side he watched the old West turn into the Midwest.

Laws prohibiting alcohol were passed, but the old wagon master paid them no mind. Then the sheriff busted him on the eve of Independence Day 1899. He was hauled off to the county seat and jailed as a common bootlegger.

Although charges were ultimately dismissed, it was clear that the wide-open days of the Santa Fe Trail had disappeared over the horizon with the last New Mexico–bound wagon train. The era of Carrie A. Nation had arrived. Carrie was the nation's leading prohibitionist and a homegrown Sunflower State product from Medicine Lodge, Kansas. To make sure the point was understood by one and all, in 1906 Parker was again arrested. These charges too stemmed from bootlegging. This time he was fined $100 and imprisoned for thirty days. He was eighty-five years old and a recent widower, having lost his wife the year before. Clearly, at least as far as Charley Parker was concerned, the good old days were a thing of the past.

PRAIRIE TSUNAMI AT POINT OF ROCKS

- 1914 -

MAY 1, 1914, WAS A DAY OF INFAMY. On that date a tsunami twelve feet high stormed down the valley. It gathered trees, cattle, and buildings into its watery bosom. Its victims tumbled head over heels. They were ground down by the abrasive action of billions of grains of sand churning in the wall of water. There was no hope of escape. In the blink of an eye, the crest of the wall of water had passed, but the damage it did wrecked lives and destroyed fortunes.

Did this devastating tidal wave occur on some distant shore, say far across the Pacific, on a south sea island? No, it happened in the very heart of the continental United States at a memorable spot on the Old Santa Fe Trail. The place is called Point of Rocks. The body of water it happened on is the Cimarron River.

The Cimarron may seem an unusual stream for such a wild, roaring water event. One old trader who wrote a book about his years in the West said he saw water running in the bed of the river only four or five times in all his years on the trail. Even though the river heads in the mountains of New Mexico and is nourished in the spring by melting snow, it was entirely possible for some freighters to have passed back and forth to Santa Fe many times without encountering a drop of water. The traders called the area around the river the Cimarron Desert, giving an idea of what the usual expectation for that river was. Today the river is designated the Dry Cimarron in New Mexico and may as well be called that in the Oklahoma panhandle and Kansas. On the other hand, the Spanish word from which the English Cimarron comes means "wild or untamed."

Old trail hand Billy Dixon heartily concurred with the sentiment that the Cimarron was an untamed river. In Oklahoma the river passed through several large expanses of salt, making its water undrinkable. Dixon claimed a mouthful of the stuff would induce nausea, and he called the Cimarron one of the most dangerous rivers on the southern plains. He said that the stream, when it was running, was frequently three or four hundred yards across. This would appear to make it a huge river, but in fact it was very shallow and sandy. Strangely enough, the sand was what made for the danger. An underflow turned the sand into quicksand. "The river grips like a vise, and the river sucks down and buries all that it touches—trees, wagons, horses, cattle, and men alike, if the latter should be too weak to extricate themselves. In the old days countless buffalo bogged down and disappeared beneath the sands of the Cimarron. Their dismembered skeletons are frequently uncovered at this day when the river is in flood."

The most dangerous time to go into the Cimarron was after a rise. As the current boils and roils along, according to Dixon, "the river loosens and hurls along an astonishing quantity of sand. Unless naked, a man quickly finds himself pulled down by the increasing weight of sand that lodges in his clothes, and swimming becomes difficult and finally impossible." Dixon said that "stripped bare, a swimmer can sustain himself in the Cimarron with greater ease than most other streams, as the salt and sand give the water extraordinary buoyancy." He added,

"No man should ever tackle the Cimarron in flood until after he has stripped to the skin and kicked off his boots. The experienced cow pony seems to realize its danger when crossing the Cimarron, taking short, quick steps and moving forward without the slightest pause. To stop would be to sink in the quicksand." Dixon advised that if one had to cross the river in flood stage, it was advisable to go in with a horse that knew how to deal with the river. As for the rider, it was best "to seize the horse's tail" and swim behind.

Dixon was well aware of the flash floods that made (and make) the Cimarron so dangerous. "A settler may cross the river at noon blinded by the clouds of sand that have been whipped up by the wind. Fifteen minutes later he finds the river roaring and thundering from bank to bank. What is known as a 'head rise,' formed by a cloud burst far out in the Plains country, has come down, a solid wall of water, often four or five feet high. Sometimes two or more or these 'head rises' follow in succession. The sand is torn loose and brought up from the very bottom of the river. To venture into the Cimarron at such times would be folly."

Santa Fe Trail freighters paralleled the Cimarron River for the best part of a hundred miles through southwestern Kansas and portions of Oklahoma, Colorado, and New Mexico. The most prominent land-mark in the stretch through Kansas was known as Point of Rocks. For one going from the mountainous west to the east, this feature would have been a rather unremarkable hogback of sandstone rising perhaps 150 feet above the river's floodplain. However, for one coming from the flat prairie, it jutted up dramatically. In 1880, the year the Santa Fe Trail passed into history, Point of Rocks changed its status too. Instead of being merely a landmark on the old trail, Point of Rocks became the headquarters of a huge cattle establishment known as Point of Rocks Ranch, the brainchild of John W. Beaty and his brothers.

John had first sighted Point of Rocks as a trail hand when he was nineteen. Like many early freighters he hailed from Missouri of Kentucky stock, his grandmother, Peggy Crockett Beaty, being the sister of Davy Crockett. Remembering the good grazing on the Cimarron River bottom and the permanent water hole at Middle Spring, not far from Point of Rocks, he and his brothers homesteaded the 160 acres around each of those places. They then went to Texas and bought cattle, which they grazed on the open prairie. They encouraged loyal employees to homestead spots suitable for farming as shown by the availability of water or good grass. The brothers would then buy these homesteads as soon as title to the land was gained. Legitimate homesteaders found trying to make a living on the allotted 160 acres of prairie tough going, and those who stuck out the mandatory five-year period frequently sold to the brothers. By 1897 the Beaty brothers had acquired eighteen thousand acres of land around Point of Rocks. In that year they sold their interest to Henry Boyce. Twelve thousand head of cattle also changed hands. At least twenty acres, and perhaps as high as forty acres, would be required to graze one head of stock. Therefore, it can be estimated that the Point of Rocks Ranch exerted control over a quarter to a half million acres of rangeland in southwest Kansas and neighboring sections of Colorado and Oklahoma at the time.

The new owner of Point of Rocks, Henry Boyce, grew up herding cattle in Las Vegas, New Mexico. Earlier in life, he had managed the famous XIT Ranch in the Texas panhandle. By the turn of the century, he had become a wheeler and dealer of national proportions with holdings in California urban real estate and Arizona ranch land, as well as Point of Rocks Ranch. In Kansas a new wave of homesteaders proved troublesome for Boyce. Boyce and other cattlemen did not believe these grangers could actually make a living on their small claims. The cattlemen felt they merely had to wait for a dry spell to allow them to buy the homesteaders out at bargain prices. Point of Rocks was extremely isolated, being seventy-five miles from a railroad, so Boyce sold his holdings to concentrate on other investments. By 1914 Point of Rocks Ranch was owned by Sam King. He lived in Hutchinson, Kansas, two hundred miles away. His representative, foreman Perry Brite, managed the operation from the ranch buildings built under the Point of Rocks bluff. Had the Beatys' chosen a less picturesque spot, not hemmed in by the bluffs, perhaps the devastation could have been avoided.

On May 1, 1914, without warning, a head rise of the sort Billy Dixon described came thundering down the valley. The ranch house trapped in the area between the riverbed and the bluffs was snatched up in the on-rushing wall of water. So too were the corrals, windmills, cattle, Model T cars, everything. The foreman Perry Brite escaped. So did his wife. Not so lucky were the couple's two children, Madge, aged thirteen, and Merle, three. They were swept up by the raging current. Days later their mangled bodies were found miles downstream, and they were buried where they lay.

The flood completely destroyed Point of Rocks Ranch. The rich bottomlands that had been harvested for prairie hay were ruined and never came back. The ranch struggled on for a while, never turning a profit. Contrary to the ranchers' expectations, farmers moved in and took over operations on the land. Using modern tractors that allowed for the tillage of large acreage, they plowed up the sod and planted wheat and other dryland grains. The farmers made money. Then came the great drought of the 1930s. The cultivated topsoil blew away. The area got a new name, the Dust Bowl, which included the portions of Colorado and Oklahoma the original Point of Rocks Ranch occupied. Morton County, where Point of Rocks Ranch headquarters was located, was the worst hit of any Dust Bowl county. Nowadays the lands around Point of Rocks are again cattle range and called the Cimarron National Grassland. Nature, whether in the way of flood or drought, could be very harsh in the land along the Old Santa Fe Trail.

UNION STATION MASSACRE

- 1933 -

THE LAST SANTA FE–BOUND WAGON TRAIN HITCHED UP and pulled out of the Westport area of Kansas City sometime after the Civil War. The wagon trains had become obsolete, because the railroads had replaced them. Not surprisingly, many of the industries that grew up in Kansas City in the intervening years were associated with transportation, especially the stockyards and meatpacking businesses. Perhaps because of this, Kansas City continued to have a frontier flavor long after the Santa Fe Trail became defunct. This claim was shown to be true on the morning of June 17, 1933. The location was Kansas City's railroad hub, known as Union Station. It was the modern successor to Westport and was only a mile away from the place where the earlier wagon trains had formed.

It should have been a fairly routine matter. Three federal agents with the help of a rural police officer were escorting an escaped convict. The agents planned to transfer the prisoner from a railroad train to an automobile for the short trip to the federal prison at Leavenworth, Kansas.

The convict was Frank "Jelly" Nash. Nash was a bank robber who worked with the Alvin "Creepy" Karpis gang. Nash's nickname came from his preference for blowing safes with nitroglycerine. Gangland slang called the substance "jelly." He had walked away from the national prison by impersonating a civilian through carrying a heavy book, the collected works of William Shakespeare. Nash then helped an additional half dozen or so convicts to escape. The federal agents, who in the slang of the time were called G-men, had learned of Nash's whereabouts when they arrested other members of his bank-robbing gang. His bank-robbing friends said Nash was living in Hot Springs, Arkansas, even more of a wide-open town than Kansas City. The G-men, with the assistance of a lawman from a county in nearby eastern Oklahoma, located Nash. They picked him up in a bookie joint, and he was whisked into an automobile and spirited out of Hot Springs.

The federal agents believed they had little chance of keeping Nash if they followed the correct procedure. If they jailed him in Hot Springs, the corrupt local officials would have thwarted them by not giving him back to federal authorities, or perhaps simply released him from jail. So in essence they kidnapped him. To make matters worse, the lawmen were spotted bundling their prisoner aboard the night train at Fort Smith, Arkansas. Some of Nash's friends telephoned Kansas City's number one crime boss, Johnny Lazia.

Lazia seemed more like a Hollywood creation than a real Mafia capo. He was surprisingly young, in his thirties. He dressed flashily in suits of the latest fashion, chewed gum continually, and hung out in the most popular Kansas City nightclubs. He had a good word for everyone, and he also was known as a big tipper. None of this masked the fact that he was a hoodlum of the worst sort. By the time he was eighteen, he had pulled his first armed robbery. He was caught and sent to prison. When he got out, he went to work organizing his Italian neighborhood politically. Using strong-arm tactics, he gained control of Kansas City's North End. Ultimately he became a political boss. Kansas City's big boss was Tom Pendergast. Pendergast allowed Lazia a free hand in the appointment of policemen, so as many as seventy-five former convicts drew policeman's pay. Lazia also demanded all visiting criminals alert him to their presence in his town. He would demand money and services from the visiting gunmen, gangsters, and killers, for which he allowed them to remain unmolested by Kansas City police.

On the Saturday evening of June 16, Charles Arthur Floyd, who had been dubbed "Pretty Boy" by the media, and Adam Richetti let Lazia know of their arrival in town. Floyd and Richetti had been accompanied by the Polk County, Missouri, sheriff, Jack Killingsworth, whom they had snatched to insure safe passage from southern Missouri. Richetti, who was an alcoholic, guzzled down an enormous quantity of booze during the trip. He frightened the sheriff by becoming progressively more drunk and psychopathic. Floyd, too, acted strangely. He lectured the sheriff on the ills of criminal justice system. But once in Kansas City, Floyd set the lawman free unharmed. He promised he would do so, and he did. Many saw "Pretty Boy" Floyd as a Robin Hood–like gangster, and actions such as his release of the sheriff just added to that aura.

Floyd grew up dirt poor in the Cookson Hills of Oklahoma. At eighteen he bought a pistol and pulled his first heist, netting $350 in pennies. His next job gained him $16,000. He bought a new car, returned to the Cookson Hills, and was promptly arrested by suspicious policemen. A search of his house turned up some of the cash in the original wrappers. He was sent away for three years. When he got out, he vowed never to return to prison. In the dozen years prior 1933, Floyd is rumored to have robbed thirty banks and to have killed ten men. One of these appears to have been the killer of his father, who had been acquitted of the charge of homicide. Floyd returned to the Cookson Hills, and his father's killer was never seen again. He killed two men for calling him "Pretty Boy" to his face. Apparently, he despised the nickname.

Adam Richetti was younger than Floyd, being only twenty-four in 1933. After a series of juvenile scrapes with the law, he became involved in a failed bank robbery in a small Oklahoma town. Vigilant townspeople shot or captured his accomplices. Richetti, though wounded, drove the getaway car into the country but was collared by the sheriff. Strangely, after his conviction, he served only four months in prison before being released. He immediately went into a crime partnership with Pretty Boy.

On learning of Floyd's presence in Kansas City, Lazia ordered him and Richetti to team up with Verne Miller, another midwestern boy. He grew up in South Dakota, where he had twice been elected county sheriff. He had also served in the army during World War I and apparently was decorated for heroism. He was also wounded and poisoned by mustard gas. Sometime during the 1920s he suddenly went "bad." He embezzled $6,000 from his own sheriff's department and ran away to Saint Paul, Minnesota, for a drinking spree. He returned to Dakota, turned himself in, and served a sentence in prison. For a time he appeared to turn over a new leaf and took up work as a mechanic. But then Miller lost it. He robbed banks and murdered people with abandon. He once shot three men to death, even though he had a reason to kill just one of them. Frank Nash had been one of his accomplices in the bank-robbing gang. Miller wanted him freed.

Kansas City's Union Station, the third largest train depot in the nation, was completed almost twenty years earlier, having been designed to serve the community for two hundred years. The train from Fort Smith carrying the lawmen and their prisoner arrived at the station at 7:15. Though in a massive building, the agents, with the shackled Nash, took just a few minutes to walk from the concourse where the train arrived to the front of the building where police cars waited for the drive to Leavenworth.

Two Kansas City police detectives met the officers and prisoner in front of Union Station. The local lawmen were not very well armed. The Kansas City cops drove what was known as a riot car, called the Hotshot. It should have carried a submachine gun, but their machine gun had mysteriously disappeared. Furthermore, the federal agents did not carry guns. Regulations at the time banned G-men from packing weapons. The prisoner was briskly shunted into the front seat of a waiting Federal Bureau of Investigation vehicle. Agents bundled into the back; other lawmen stood nervously around the car waiting for it to zoom off. Then out of nowhere Miller, Richetti, and Floyd, toting submachine guns, appeared. They confronted the law officers, demanding Nash.

A gun battle broke out at point-blank range. Two minutes later five men, four law enforcement agents and Jelly Nash, were dead, and the would-be liberators had disappeared as quickly and mysteriously as they had arrived.

Ironically, modern investigators have shown that most or all of the dead were killed by police weapons. Agent Joe Lackey, in the backseat of the bureau's car, seems to have grabbed the first available shooting iron and blazed away. That weapon was a scattergun that Oklahoma lawman Otto Reed specially prepared. The ball bearings the rural police officer loaded the shells with scattered far and wide, getting friend and foe alike. Sheriff Reed sat next to Lackey, and when Lackey blazed away, the sheriff was killed along with the prisoner in the front seat and the agent driving. The other two dead men, Kansas City police officers, may also have fallen from the shotgun's pellets, or they may have been hit by the criminals' submachine guns. In any case, from start to finish, the gun battle lasted about thirty seconds.

The aftereffects shocked the nation and made for startling changes. J. Edgar Hoover, the head of the FBI, demanded the authority to retool his relatively obscure agency into a national detective force complete with armed agents. The infamy of the bloodbath made the three purported shooters too hot for anyone to risk hiding. All were run to ground within about a year.

Miller was killed by other criminals in Detroit in the fall of 1933. Floyd and Richetti fled to Buffalo, New York. They lived quietly in a safe-haven apartment for many months. In the fall of 1934, they decided to return to the Midwest. Floyd got no farther than Ohio, where he was gunned down on a farmstead much like the one he started life on in Oklahoma. During his last hours Floyd confirmed his reputation as a gentleman bandit. He found a car at a farm with keys in the ignition. Rather than simply steal the car, he asked the housewife for a ride. The woman refused to help him. Though armed and capable of taking it by force, he simply walked away. The police were called. He was cornered in a cornfield and shot and killed. His body was buried in Oklahoma, and more than ten thousand attended his funeral. It is claimed to have been the largest funeral in the state's history.

Richetti was also captured in Ohio, but he was brought back to Missouri. Much legal wrangling occurred before he finally went on trial. The authorities wanted to make sure the strongest case possible was put forth. Finally, he was tried, convicted, and condemned to death. This time he was not released from prison after a short period of incarceration. He was executed in October of 1938, more than five years after the Kansas City massacre.

His death was among the last of the repercussions of that event. Johnny Lazia had been assassinated in front of his residence about a year after the massacre. It is claimed the submachine gun that killed him had been used in the Union Station shooting. Federal agents also convicted many other minor players in the event. Within a few years, they even managed to put Boss Tom Pendergast himself behind bars.

SANTA FE'S LA FONDA

- 1968 -

THE ADOBE BUILDING JUST OFF THE PLAZA IN SANTA FE was large, cathedral like. The women inside the main chamber were dressed like nuns. They acted like nuns too, talking demurely among themselves. They had been strictly trained: None of them was ever known to laugh loudly in the main hall. They rarely smiled there, and they never burst in with questions while guests were talking to each other. When not occupied with their normal duties, the women waxed the exposed wood surfaces. They waxed them until they shone, and then they worked on the silver, polishing and repolishing it until it sparkled. Old habits died hard. Even today—the last day of operation—the women staff, known as Harvey Girls, worked hard at making the establishment, the Harvey House in the La Fonda Hotel, as clean and shiny as the morning it opened years before.

Deprivation had been the lot of the Santa Fe Trail freighter. His fare for the six-week trip across the prairie amounted to about fifty pounds of bacon, the same amount of flour, ten pounds of coffee, and twenty of sugar. When not on the buffalo range, the old team-ster rarely had fresh meat. Odd, indeed was it, that the most elegant food served in the annals of American travel would occur on the Old Santa Fe Trail, and just shortly after the last teams of mules were replaced by the iron horse.

The person responsible for this turn of events was an English-man, Fred Harvey. He arrived in the United States as an orphan at the age of fifteen. He first worked as a busboy in a New York cafe, making $2 a week. Then followed jaunts in a New Orleans restau-rant, and finally at the age of twenty-two, he opened his own place in Saint Louis. The Saint Louis cafe failed when he fell out with his partner on account of the slavery issue. The partner ran off with the cash receipts, and Fred moved farther west and got a job in the so-called moving post office sorting mail in a railroad car. He was one of the first two people ever employed to do such work. The twin goal posts of Fred Harvey's life had been set, restaurant work and railroading.

For the next fifteen years, he progressed his way up through the Chicago, Burlington, and Quincy Railroad hierarchy, becoming their western freight manager. On the side he attempted to run, with a partner, a couple of railroad cafes on the Kansas Pacific line. He asked his CB&Q boss if he could put a restaurant in one of the company depots. The boss, seeing no need for such an enterprise, suggested he try the Atchison, Topeka, and Santa Fe Railroad.

Santa Fe officials held an entirely different view of commissary operations. An 1876 excursion train had given them an object lesson. This special run had celebrated the arrival of the line in Pueblo, Col-orado. It was supposed to take thirty-six hours to go from Topeka to Pueblo, and then return, taking a mere three days. Almost five hun-dred people were packed into the railcars for the tour across the plains. Everyone was supposed to bring food for the trip. However, the tempestuous prairie climate served up a late-spring snowstorm. The train slowed to a crawl and arrived in Pueblo a day late. A trainload of famished passengers descended on the small population of the village like a horde of locusts—and precious little was there to feed them. Despite this glitch the excursion was regarded as a success by all involved. Santa Fe teamsters could not have performed a similar feat, crossing the plains and returning, in two months. Still, the exposed underbelly of railroad passenger operations had been shown.

Fred Harvey's request to AT&SF officials, shortly thereafter, regarding a station restaurant was greeted with enthusiasm. The "restaurant" in fact turned out to be a second-story lunchroom in the Topeka depot. Fred and his manager scoured the dingy eatery until squeaky clean, and then they ordered new linen and revamped the menu. Within weeks the place was doing a capacity business. The president of the Santa Fe, thanks to the disastrous Pueblo excursion, understood the value of feeding his passengers. He gave Fred leave to establish eateries in all Santa Fe depots. The railroad agreed to provide free passage for Fred's employees and provisions. It also agreed to give the restaurants ice and coal, for no charge. All this was done with a handshake, as only two written contracts for small operations appear ever to have been drawn up.

By the late 1880s, less than ten years after the end of the Santa Fe Trail with its Indian wars and blizzards, Fred Harvey eateries had been established every one hundred miles along AT&SF. And Fred Harvey made this promise to his customers: "Where the name Fred Harvey appears, the traveling public expects much. It may be in the desert a hundred miles from water, but if it is a Fred Harvey place, you get filtered spring water, ice, fresh fruit and every other good thing you can find at the same season in the best places in New York or Chicago. How the miracle occurs, you do not know—it is a Fred Harvey concern—that is enough."

"Meals by Fred Harvey," as they were known, were not cheap. They cost 75 cents. The kitchen and dining room help, by contrast, made from $10 to $15 a month. But the food was plentiful, and the menu ritzy. Bluepoint oysters or artichokes a la Grecque might furnish the first course. Consomme bellevue or petite marmite could be the soup. Medallion of salmon poche, jumbo bullfrog almondienne, or fried soft-shelled crabs, among many other choices, provided the fish course. Entrees might include milk-fed chicken a l'Espagnole au risotto or calf's sweetbreads belle Helene. Dessert might be a charlotte russe, petits fours, or more familiar fare such as chocolate layer cake. The food was coordinated so passengers would not be presented with similar menus on their travels. And Fred Harvey restaurants had atmosphere. Men had to wear coats in the dining room, and proper decorum was maintained by all, customers as well as employees.

A meal stop lasted exactly thirty minutes. Railroad employees telegraphed ahead the number of diners and their menu choices. When the train pulled into the station, a gong sounded, and the passengers were escorted to the dining room, where the food was ready and waiting to be served. Afterward, there would usually be enough time to buy a cigar from the Fred Harvey newsstand—at two to four times the regular price—and to check out the Indian crafts that Fred Harvey carried in many of his gift shops. One of the chain's notable achievements was providing cash money to Indians for their handiwork. Anthropologists owe thanks to Fred Harvey for saving many artifacts that might otherwise have perished. The anthropological aspect of the Fred Harvey chain may be its most noteworthy long-term effect.

All this required military precision and efficiency, and Fred Harvey ran his many restaurants like a general. He routinely inspected every one of his establishments—on a surprise basis. He ran his handkerchief over out-of-the-way woodwork. Grease or dust marks would cause a tremor among the help, and probably a dismissal. Employees with bad attitudes were fired on the spot. Cracked or chipped dishes were discarded.

A Las Vegas, New Mexico, manager, tired of his waiters carousing and causing trouble, sacked the lot in 1883. In their place he hired women. Fred Harvey liked the way the experiment worked out. He began replacing all of his wait help with women. Staff at many locations numbered as high as fifty employees. At the top stood the manager with the chef just below him. Then there were several assistant cooks, a butcher, a baker, pantry girls, and twenty-five or more waitresses. Providing quarters for all those single women in remote locations was a challenge. But Harvey, with his military system, was prepared for it. The women were hired from throughout the country through recruiting offices in Kansas City and Chicago. Special dormitories were constructed. Housemothers supervised the personal lives of the women. As with everything else, Fred Harvey demanded strict standards in the education and deportment of his female employees. They had to be well educated with a high school degree preferable. Women had to agree not to marry for the period of their contract, usually a year. After their contracts expired, many Harvey girls married local men and stayed to raise families. It was said, tongue in cheek, that Fred Harvey civilized and populated the Southwest.

Harvey employees, though fearful of the company standards, remained fiercely loyal, many staying on for years and years. The pay was better than average and the benefits were really superb. Room and board were provided by the company, and a free ticket on the Santa Fe line, along with meals and lodging, insured an expense-paid vacation every year.

Fred Harvey died in 1901. His last words supposedly were "Don't cut the ham too thin," indicative of the luxuriant style of his restaurants and hotels. The company was taken over by his sons, who continued in his tradition. Just as the AT&SF replaced the Old Santa Fe Trail, new technologies began impinging on the Harvey houses. By the 1930s dining cars had made the necessity for in-place eating establishments in far-flung locations obsolete. And air traffic and the automobile were threatening rail passenger traffic. In the 1940s and 1950s, most of the Harvey restaurants (and hotels, for Harvey ran hotels too) were boarded up.

Ironically, one of the last establishments added to the Harvey line was La Fonda in Santa Fe. Owing to Santa Fe's geographical location in an out-of-the-way mountain valley, the AT&SF mainline passed through Lamy, New Mexico, seventeen miles away. It wasn't until the 1920s that the Santa Fe railway acquired the luxury hotel, which was believed to be the oldest site for a hotel in North America. An inn of one kind or another is believed to have occupied the spot since 1610. Among other names, it had been called the Exchange Hotel and managed by old trail hand Charles Parker for a time before the Civil War. The 147-room La Fonda was the crown jewel in the Harvey hospitality empire in the mid-twentieth century. Ownership passed to other hands in 1968. Fittingly, it was among the very last of the Harvey Houses, which did so much to civilize life along the Old Santa Fe Trail, to close.

THE FINAL CHAPTER:
"THE SANTA FE TRAIL LIVES ON"

- 1986 -

It had been tried many times before.

About every twenty years people got together and made an effort. They had done it in 1910, 1928, 1948, and 1960–1961. All ended in failure.

Every attempt to develop an organization devoted to the Santa Fe Trail had fizzled out. The 1928 venture had as its head the future president of the United States, Harry S Truman. The organization was called the National Old Trails Road Association. But this attempt and others flopped because the scope of their organizations was too narrow. Future President Truman's group, for instance, was mainly interested in seeing that a modern hard-surfaced road was completed along the old trails in the area. When asphalt or concrete roadways became common, the organization was no longer needed.

The stakes, for those who believe the past is the surest guide to the future, were high. So in 1986 they tried again. This time, thanks to the bringing together of the best possible people for the effort—and a measure of luck—it worked.

Like the earlier ventures the 1986 one started with a limited scope. In 1984 Joy Poole, the administrator for the Colorado Historical Society's Baca House and Bloom Mansion's museum in Trinidad, Colorado, persuaded her organization to sponsor a Santa Fe Trail conference. Trinidad stands at the foot of Raton Pass. Uncle Dick Wootton's tollgate had been situated several miles south of the town. As such, it was one of a handful of "natural" sites for such a gathering. Her idea was to invite personnel from museums along the route of the trail. In order to make the event interesting, noted trail scholars would be invited to make presentations.

Ms. Poole wrote Ruth Olson of the Santa Fe Trail Center in Larned, Kansas. The Trail Center, just west of the town of Larned, was one of the local museums Ms. Poole hoped to interest in her conference. She asked for names of trail scholars. Ms. Olson suggested Poole contact Dr. Marc Simmons, who lived near Santa Fe. Even then, he was regarded as the leading historian in matters regarding the Santa Fe Trail and the Southwest. Dr. Simmons said he would be happy to help. He said he believed involving the very best people was the key to making a top-rate conference. Here's a list of those he suggested be included on the scholarly program.

- Jack D. Rittenhouse, owner of the Stagecoach Press in Santa Fe, New Mexico. Rittenhouse specialized in reprinting books written about the old West.

- David Dary, professor at the University of Kansas. Dary had wide experience in journalism of all kinds, having worked for CBS and NBC in Texas and Washington, D.C., before taking a position at the university. His many books about the West established him as one of the best-known writers on trans-Missouri history.

- Dr. Leo E. Oliva, former professor at Fort Hays State University. Dr. Oliva knew the land along the trail and its scholarship. After teaching for fifteen years at the university, he assumed management of the family wheat farm. Dr. Oliva was a leading scholar of frontier military history, having written more than a half dozen books on the topic.

- Dr. Sandra Myers, a PhD from Texas Christian University. Dr. Myers had published books on many aspects of the West, and she was invited to talk about the feminine experience on the Santa Fe Trail.

- David Lavender, a high school teacher in California for many years. His spare time was devoted to writing books on the historical West. His *Bent's Fort* was nominated for the Pulitzer Prize and was on everyone's short list for one of the best books ever about the Santa Fe Trail. He was a natural.

Somehow, Joy Poole's vision expanded. Why go to all this work for just one meeting? After corresponding with Marc, she visited him at his home in Cerrillos, New Mexico. When Joy and Marc put their heads together, the idea for a full-fledged Santa Fe Trail Association was hatched. Understanding that the earlier efforts had failed for lack of a broad general mission, Joy and Marc, with the help of others, sought to include all classes of people with an interest in the trail. Those interested in determining the exact route of the trail, such as Ralph Hathaway of Chase, Kansas, on whose farm are some of the finest remnants of Santa Fe Trail ruts, were to be honored at the first meeting. A man who was interested in trail technology was put forth for the board of the fledgling organization. The man, Mark L. Gardner, studied the evolution of the freight wagon on the trail. Those whose interests were all the old trails of the West, such as Gregory Franzwa, were invited to attend and thanked for their help.

And finally, the meeting, which originally was intended for museum personnel, was opened to the general public. The dates were set for September 12 and 13, 1986. Would anyone come?

A multitude attended. In all, 230 people signed up—from all five states that the Santa Fe Trail passed through. Most had never attended an academic conference. But interested in the trail, they were drawn by the full range of offerings, panel discussions, formal lectures, tours, and other events. They wanted to see a trail organization formed. Joy Poole, showing her usual foresight, had incorporated the organization. She also had developed a fallback position by approaching the Oregon-California Trail Association about affiliating with it as a subsidiary organization.

But a great deal of talent was assembled in Trinidad. And it was highly motivated—so far as the Santa Fe Trail was concerned. Almost immediately, it became apparent that the Santa Fe Trail Council (its first name) would stand on its own feet. The backbone of any organization is communication, especially true of one devoted to history. Dr. Leo Oliva volunteered to edit a newsletter, which would simultaneously keep the members up to date and provide a forum for new trail information.

A second meeting was scheduled for the following year. The capable Barbara Peirce of Hutchinson, Kansas, undertook to host it. But who would be the president of this new organization? At the time the issue may have seemed in doubt, but in retrospect there was only one right person for the job. That person was Marc Simmons.

He had gotten his PhD in history in 1965 from the University of New Mexico. But he was far from a scholar in an ivory tower. He might better be called a writer in an adobe silo. While finishing graduate classes at the university, Marc bought some acreage in the hills around Santa Fe. Using his own hands, he molded clay into adobe bricks and built a one-room cabin. Later, he added two rooms to the house and erected a small guesthouse and a stable. His home was lighted then (and even now) by kerosene lanterns, and his writing was done on a manual typewriter. His two accommodations to the modern world were a small television, which he powered using his pickup truck battery, and a telephone.

After graduation he set himself up as an independent historian and freelance writer. Dr. Simmons lived the way he did because he wanted to write about southwestern history from the point of view of those who really lived it. Earlier, he had bought a burro and, using the animal as pack stock, had hiked many of the old trails of New Mexico. One could hardly do New Mexican history without a fluent knowledge of Spanish. Although he had been taking Spanish since middle school, he traveled to Guanajuato, Mexico, for an intensive course. His many books on the Spanish experience in the Southwest were the result. Another result was his induction into the Order of Isabel la Catolica, by invitation of King Juan Carlos I of Spain. Essentially, he had been knighted for his work on the history of Spain in the New World.

But more importantly so far as western history goes, Marc had ridden the range as a real cowboy. He'd even taken part in a real cattle drive from the North Platte to Medicine Bow National Forest in Wyoming—for the princely sum of $100 a month. After he had earned his PhD, he completed requirements for a certificate and farrier license. As many writers have done when starting out, Marc subsidized his writing by working. Not many, though, worked as a farrier, that is shoeing horses. He also became a blacksmith and produced one of his best-loved books, *Southwestern Colonial Ironwork: The Spanish Blacksmithing Tradition from Texas to California*.

In other words, Marc was a man who got to the bottom of his subject and knew it inside out. He had already traveled the Santa Fe Trail six or seven times and had written six books about the trail. In truth, he was also—with the help and encouragement of Joy Poole—the person who made the organization happen. He was the right man as president. Marc's determination to make the idea work—and his grit—were tremendous. They were shown when he was seriously injured in an accident during his first year as president. He spent months recuperating, but still he appeared at the second meeting on crutches and delivered a stirring trail lecture.

The Santa Fe Trail Association is now in its third decade. It operates on many fronts, not the least of which is the amazing amount of material about the trail and the times that it has developed. Some of this material is in the newsletter *Wagon Tracks* and some of it is online (www.santafetrail.org) and through chapter Web sites. The first president closed his talk in Trinidad with a remark that is certainly true, thanks to the association. Marc Simmons said, "The Santa Fe Trail lives on."

TRAIL TRIVIA

Captain William Becknell, the "Father of the Santa Fe Trail," was the first to drive a wagon to Santa Fe. He paid $150 for it in Missouri and sold the vehicle in New Mexico for $700. Becknell took $3,000 in goods to Santa Fe on his second trip. He sold the lot for $60,000. Fanny Marshall, a local Missourian, invested $60 in this venture. Becknell paid her $900. In 1824 Meredith Marmaduke freighted $30,000 in goods across the plains. He returned with $180,000 in gold, silver, furs, and mules.

William Becknell may have been the "Father of the Santa Fe Trail," but Senator Thomas Hart Benton was its grandfather. From the very start Senator Benton took an interest in and promoted the trade. He commissioned a report on the trail's opportunities by the trader Augustus Storrs. In the early days of the United States, Congress was extremely stingy about appropriating money for "internal improvements." Nevertheless, Benton saw that federal money was granted to survey and mark the road to Santa Fe. Among other things, the commissioners, including George Sibley, were to conclude treaties with the Osage and Kansas Indians allowing for safe passage of traders. Later, Benton was responsible for the stationing of troops on the trail when Indian depredations began to occur.

In the early days of the trade, the Conestoga wagon, already in use throughout the country, was the standard trail wagon. The Conestoga was developed in Pennsylvania about the time of the Revolutionary

War. Apparently, its name came from the Conestoga River. It was influenced by wagon designs from Germany and England and had slanting end gates and an overarching canvas tilt or cover. The wagon box bowed in the middle, the bow allowing for bulk cargo such as grain to "self-center," keeping the load, which could weigh up to two and a half tons, balanced. Wagon wheels were lubricated frequently by a combination of tallow and pine pitch. A bucket of this mixture with a dauber hung from the wagon. The front yoke of draft animals, mules or oxen, were called the leaders. The rear set was known as wheelers, and the middle yoke or yokes, the swing team(s). Animals were directed by whips and calls. Supposedly gee would induce the team to turn right, haw, to the left, and whoa would cause them to halt.

Santa Fe–bound wagons made their way to Council Grove, Kansas, in small groups. There they formed into caravans for the passage across the plains. The average Santa Fe–bound train had about two dozen wagons. At Council Grove the owners or operators of the wagons elected a captain called a wagon master or conductor. The conductor had the responsibility to see to the security and other arrangements for the train, but he had very little means to enforce his decisions. A typical train of two dozen or so wagons required up to three dozen men to manage it properly. A teamster was in charge of each wagon. He was called a bull whacker if the vehicle was ox powered or a mule skinner if the wagon was mule drawn. Two or three herders looked after the extra stock, which amounted to thirty to forty animals used as replacements for worn-out or injured critters. The men were organized into messes of about eight men. One man usually took on the role of cook, and the others washed up, gathered firewood, and so on. When traversing hostile areas, each man stood guard half the night every other night. Indian attack was most likely to come just before or at dawn.

In the early days Missouri traders did not often carry gunpowder, candlewick, iron, lead, tobacco, or shoes to New Mexico. These items were forbidden or prohibitively taxed in order to keep them out of the hands of the populace. Luxury items were reserved for the upper classes, and it was feared the availability of gunpowder and lead could possibly lead to rebellion. Sometimes silver and gold could not be exported, according to Mexican law. Other times a tax needed to be paid for their export. In any event, many traders smuggled hard currency back to Missouri.

In the years prior to the Civil War, it cost $8 to $10 to ship a hundred pounds to Santa Fe over the trail or about 1 cent per pound per hundred miles. During the Civil War the price climbed to about $15, reflecting the high price of labor and Indian troubles.

Dr. John Sappington invented Sappington's Anti-Fever Pills. His great-great-great-granddaughter was Ginger Rogers, a famous movie star in the 1930s and 1940s.

The Santa Fe Trail passed through five states: Missouri, Kansas, Oklahoma, Colorado, and New Mexico. More than half of the trail ran through Kansas.

The Santa Fe trader Meredith Miles Marmaduke was for a short time governor of Missouri. Today, most people would call him politically enlightened. He was the first governor to propose laws to help people with mental illness. At a great personal and political cost, he opposed slavery. Ironically, while a trader on the Santa Fe Trail, he may have been the first to incite the Indians against the freighters. After two of his party were killed while peaceably napping, he allowed his men to open unprovoked hostilities against the next group of Indians encountered. From the friendly actions of these Indians, it is unlikely they were guilty of the murders.

The creek where Don Antonio Chavez was killed by John McDaniel in Kansas was called Owl Creek. After his murder it was changed to Chavez Creek. Today, on maps this stream is known as Jarvis Creek, evidently a corruption of Chavez's name.

The first Fourth of July celebration in New Mexico occurred in 1831. A Santa Fe–bound wagon train paused for the day. The celebration was marked by firing off revolvers.

The trail probably had a great influence on the development of the nineteenth-century American army. Unlike today, the armed forces of our country at that time were extremely limited. For instance, in 1837, America's land-based armed forces amounted to fewer than eight thousand men, mostly employed on the western frontier. The first detachment stationed on the Arkansas River in the summer of 1829, commanded by Captain Bennet Riley, was infantry. Only officers had horses, and this foot-powered force was completely inadequate for the job of controlling the highly skilled and highly mobile plains Indians. Cavalry were not sent because the U.S. Army had no cavalry units in 1829. By 1834 the army was dispatching companies of dragoons to the plains. *Dragoon* is the name for infantry riding horses. Ultimately, the dragoon companies morphed into a full-fledged cavalry, that is, soldiers trained to maneuver and fight on horseback.

The most famous early book about the Santa Fe Trail is *Commerce of the Prairies,* written by a man who called himself Dr. Josiah Gregg. After making several trips across the prairie and netting considerable money from trading, Gregg became a scientific explorer of the Southwest and Mexico. He sent many botanical and geological specimens back to scientists in the States for further study. In those days a person often assumed a title because of his status in society rather than his actually having obtained it through traditional channels. For instance, "Colonel" A. P. Chouteau rose no higher than ensign (second lieutenant) in the army, but he was called colonel by everyone, including military men, because of his prominence. "Doctor" John Sappington had attended medical school, but he didn't actually graduate. Gregg himself applied to study with Dr. Sappington and was rejected. It was long believed Gregg had simply given himself the title of doctor because of his scholarly activity, but research shows that, after retiring from the Santa Fe trade as a middle-age adult, Gregg studied medicine in Kentucky and received the degree. He was later killed in California when abandoned by the party he was traveling with. In spite of mounting snowfall, he refused to quit his scientific investigations and continued into a treacherous range of mountains.

When President Polk provoked war with Mexico, he wanted a "little war." It was his belief that big wars gave presidents black eyes in history. He also wanted to acquire the Southwest including California for the United States. In order to accomplish all this with as little fighting as possible, it is believed he sent the Santa Fe trader James Magoffin, Susan Magoffin's brother-in-law, to Santa Fe with money to bribe Governor Manuel Armijo. In any case Armijo, who was himself a Santa Fe Trail trader, surrendered New Mexico without a shot being fired. But Polk's desire to avoid a large conflict with Mexico was thwarted. A lengthy war erupted. The United States was castigated as an aggressor nation in Europe and in history. Today, American historians look favorably on Polk for having added vast sections of the Southwest to the country, but his methods are not well regarded.

Russell, Majors and Waddell was the biggest freight company on the Santa Fe Trail in the years before and after the Civil War. The company paid its men well at about $30 per month with food being provided. However, the men had to sign a pledge not to swear, drink alcohol, or beat their animals. All who worked for Russell, Majors and Waddell took the oath, but it was practically impossible for a mule skinner or bull whacker to observe it faithfully. Reins were not employed in the driving of the wagons. It was believed that cursing was necessary to direct the animals. In fact, the animals were controlled by the use of whips. Outside of earshot of Russell, Majors and Waddell officers, their freighters cursed with the best of them.

The "Father of the Santa Fe Trail," William Becknell, took his men through the mountains to New Mexico. This branch of the trail, although used occasionally by packhorse trains, was forsaken by wagon travelers until 1846, when a vehicle passage was opened by General Stephen Kearney. He hoped to skirt a supposed Mexican force waiting along the Cimarron route and take New Mexico by surprise. This route was much used during and following the Civil War years when the Comanche and Kiowa were active in the Cimarron Desert and points south and west.

Daniel Boone died in 1820 near Saint Louis. Several of his descendants operated along the trail. The Hays House restaurant in Council Grove, Kansas, which is still in business, was started by Seth Hays in 1846. A great-grandson of Daniel Boone, Hays was a junior partner in an enterprise operated by A. G. Boone of the trail town of

Westport, Missouri. Nathan Boone, Daniel's son, discovered the salt spring that drew settlers to the area where the Santa Fe Trail began.

The most famous novel set along the Santa Fe Trail is probably Willa Cather's *Death Comes for the Archbishop.* Cather took as her model Bishop Jean Lamy, who first traveled the trail in 1852 when he arrived in New Mexico to become bishop of Santa Fe. On one of his trips, he brought nuns from the east. The wagon train was attacked by Comanche Indians in Kansas. Then in Colorado many of the nuns contracted cholera and died. The burial site for those nuns is unknown and a subject of controversy even today.

In 1929 Judge Harry S Truman, president of the National Old Trails Association, dedicated a granite Madonna of the Trails statue in Lexington, Missouri. The statute, paid for by the Daughters of the American Revolution, shows a mother in scoop bonnet carrying a child in her arms with another by her side. Identical statues were placed in Council Grove, Kansas; Lamar, Colorado; Boise City, Oklahoma; and Albuquerque, New Mexico.

A small cave in the side of a ravine in Council Grove was claimed as residence by an Italian priest in 1863. Born Giovanni Agostini, he was called Father Francesco along the trail. It is believed he was the son of an Italian noble. After receiving holy orders, he disgraced himself by falling in love, so he fled to the United States and worked his way west to the Santa Fe Trail during the Civil War. After accompanying a wagon train to Las Vegas, New Mexico, walking the entire 550 miles, he took up residence in another cave, whittling religious ornaments and reputedly working miracles. He was mysteriously murdered in 1869 in the Organ Mountains of New Mexico. Hermit's Peak near Las Vegas is named for him.

The most famous Santa Fe Trail landmark in Colorado was Bent's Old Fort. William Bent married a Cheyenne Indian by the name of Owl Woman. During the Mexican-American War, the army used his fort as a staging ground for the march on New Mexico. After the war Bent presented the army with a bill for services rendered. When the bill wasn't paid, Bent abandoned the post himself and blew the structure up to prevent further use by the army.

One of the most unusual mountain men and Santa Fe Trail hands was an African American by the name of James Beckwourth. He seemed to be in many places where important things happened, such as at the Sand Creek Massacre. His memoirs are among the most readable left by early residents of the West. Until recently they were regarded with suspicion, but scholarship has shown his accounts are quite accurate.

Dodge City, Kansas, is one of the most famous of all western towns, and for justifiable reasons. Many points seemed to converge at or near Dodge City. It straddles the hundredth meridian, the boundary line in the early days between Mexico and the United States. The Arkansas River, on which it is located, formed the east-west boundary between the two nations. The so-called Wet and Dry Routes of the trail met near where the town developed. Three forts were established in the area, Fort Mann, Fort Atkinson, and Fort Dodge. Even before the Atchison, Topeka, and Santa Fe Railroad arrived, it was the center for buffalo hunters decimating the great herds. The city had the longest run of any Kansas cow town. Herds were driven there from Texas from 1873 to 1885. Even today, Fort Dodge, located five miles east of the city, is employed as a home for retired military men.

In 1844 Albert Speyer attempted a dangerous winter crossing of the trail. A blizzard caught him on the Cimarron River in present-day southwest Kansas. Three hundred mules froze to death, but he managed to save his train from plundering. More mules were obtained, and he continued on toward Chihuahua, Mexico. On the way Navajos raided him and again his mules were stolen. For several seasons afterwards trail hands camping at Middle Spring amused themselves by arranging the skulls of his mules in various patterns.

After the Civil War the Thirty-eighth Infantry, and the Ninth and Tenth Calvary were stationed at many frontier posts along the Santa Fe Trail. These units were comprised of buffalo soldiers, the name given African American units. The term, originally coined by the Indians, at first was considered derogatory, but as the black soldiers came to know the buffalo and its characteristics, they adopted the term themselves. In many ways the buffalo soldiers were the best and most reliable troops on the frontier, having the lowest desertion rate, the best discipline, and the highest reenlistment. They fought valiantly in many actions up through the Spanish-American War in 1898.

BIBLIOGRAPHY

Abert, James William. *Expedition to the Southwest: An 1845 Reconnaissance of Colorado, New Mexico, Texas and Oklahoma.* Lincoln: University of Nebraska Press, 1999.

Allyn, Joseph Pratt. *West by Southwest: Letters of Joseph Pratt Allyn, a Traveller along the Santa Fe Trail, 1863.* Edited by David K. Strate. Dodge City, Kans.: Kansas Heritage House, 1984.

Arnold, Sam'l P. *Eating Up the Santa Fe Trail.* Golden, Colo.: Fulcrum Publishing, 2001.

Bent, George. *The Life of George Bent: Written from his Letters.* Edited by George Bent and Savoie Lottinville. Norman: University of Oklahoma Press, 1968.

Boyle, Susan Calafate. *Los Capitalistas: Hispano Merchants and the Santa Fe Trade.* Albuquerque: University of New Mexico, 1997.

Bauer, K. Jack. *The Mexican War: 1846–1848.* Lincoln: University of Nebraska Press, 1974.

Carson, Christopher. *Kit Carson's Autobiography.* Lincoln: University of Nebraska Press, 1966.

Cather, Willa. *Death Comes for the Archbishop.* New York: Vintage Books, 1927.

Chalfant, William Y. *Dangerous Passage: The Santa Fe Trail and the Mexican War.* Norman: University of Oklahoma Press, 1994.

Dary, David. *The Santa Fe Trail: Its History, Legends and Lore.* New York: Alfred A. Knopf, 2001.

Davis, W. W. H. *El Gringo: New Mexico and Her People.* Lincoln: University of Nebraska Press, 1982.

Densmore, Frances. *How Indians Use Wild Plants for Food and Medicine.* New York: Dover Publications, 1974.

Dixon, Olive K. *The Life of Billy Dixon.* Abilene, Tex.: State House Press, 1987.

Draper, Lyman C. *The Life of Daniel Boone.* Mechanicsburg, Pa.: Stackpole Books, 1998.

Duffus, R. L. *The Santa Fe Trail.* Albuquerque: University of New Mexico, 1972.

Ewers, John C. *Plains Indian History and Culture: Essays in Continuity and Change.* Norman: University of Oklahoma Press, 1997.

Faragher, John Mack. *Daniel Boone: The Life and Legend of an American Pioneer.* New York: Henry Holt and Company, 1992.

Favour, Alpheus H. *Old Bill Williams, Mountain Man.* Norman: University of Oklahoma Press, 1962.

Fehrenbach, T. R. *Comanches: Destruction of a People.* New York: Da Capo Press, 1994.

Ferrrell, Robert H. *Truman & Pendergast.* Columbia: University of Missouri Press, 1999.

Field, Matt. *Matt Field on the Santa Fe Trail.* Collected by Clyde and Mae Reed Porter. Norman: University of Oklahoma Press, 1995.

Foley, William E. *A History of Missouri: 1673 to 1820.* Columbia: University of Missouri Press, 1999.

Foreman, Grant. *Pioneer Days in the Early Southwest.* Lincoln: University of Nebraska Press, 1994.

Franzwa, Gregory. *Images of the Santa Fe Trail.* Saint Louis, Mo.: The Patrice Press, 1988.

————. *The Santa Fe Trail Revisited.* Saint Louis, Mo.: The Patrice Press, 1989.

Freiberger, Harriet. *Lucien Maxwell: Villain or Visionary.* Santa Fe, N.Mex.: Sunstone Press, 1999.

Garrard, Lewis H. *Wah-to-yah and the Taos Trail.* Norman: University of Oklahoma Press, 1955.

Goff, William A. "Meredith Miles Marmaduke." *The Westport Historical Quarterly* 6, no.1 (June 1970): 19–24.

Gregg, Josiah. *Commerce of the Prairies.* Norman: University of Oklahoma Press, 1954.

Grinnell. George Bird. *By Cheyenne Campfires.* Lincoln: University of Nebraska Press, 1971.

Hafen, Leroy R., ed. *French Fur Traders & Voyageurs in the American West.* Lincoln: University of Nebraska Press, 1997.

Hall, Thomas B. *Medicine on the Santa Fe Trail.* Arrow Rock: Morningside Bookshop, 1987.

Hoig, Stan. *A Travel Guide to the Plains Indians Wars.* Albuquerque: University of New Mexico, 2006.

————. *The Sand Creek Massacre.* Norman: University of Oklahoma Press, 1961.

———. *Tribal Wars of the Southern Plains.* Norman: University of Oklahoma Press, 1993.

Horgon, Paul. *Josiah Gregg and His Vision of the Early West.* New York: Farrar, Straus and Giroux, 1941.

Humphrey, Loren. *Quinine and Quarantine: Missouri Medicine through the Years.* Columbia: University of Missouri Press, 2000.

Hurt, R. Douglas. *Nathan Boone and the American Frontier.* Columbia: University of Missouri Press, 1998.

Hyde, George E. *Indians of the High Plains: From the Prehistoric Period to the Coming of the Europeans.* Norman: University of Oklahoma Press, 1959.

———. *The Pawnee Indians.* Norman: University of Oklahoma Press, 1974.

Hyslop, Stephen G. *Bound for Santa Fe.* Norman: University of Oklahoma Press, 2002.

Jones, Horace. *The Story of Early Rice County.* Lyons, Kans.: Daily News, 1959.

———. *Up from the Sod.* Lyons, Kans.: Rice County Historical Society, 1968.

Kavanagh, Thomas W. *The Comanches: A History, 1706–1875.* Lincoln: University of Nebraska Press, 1996.

Kenner, Charles L. *The Comanchero Frontier: A History of New Mexico-Plains Indian Relations.* Norman: University of Oklahoma Press, 1969.

Lane, Lydia Spencer. *I Married a Soldier.* Albuquerque: University of New Mexico, 1988.

Launius, Roger D. *Alexander William Doniphan: Portrait of a Missouri Moderate.* Columbia: University of Missouri Press, 1997.

Lavender, David. *Bent's Fort.* Lincoln: University of Nebraska Press, 1972.

Lowie, Robert H. *Indians of the Plains.* Lincoln: University of Nebraska Press, 1954.

Macfarlan, Allan and Paulette. *Handbook of American Indian Games.* New York: Dover Publications, 1959.

Marcy, Randolph B. *The Prairie Traveler.* Bedford, Mass.: Applewood Books, 1993.

Marmaduke, Meredith M. "M. M. Marmaduke Journal." *Missouri Historical Review* 6, no. 1 (October 1911): 1–10.

Magoffin, Susan Shelby. *Down the Santa Fe Trail and into Mexico: The Diaries of Susan Shelby Magoffin.* Edited by Stella M. Drumm. Lincoln: University of Nebraska Press, 1982.

Marshall, James. *Santa Fe: The Railroad That Built an Empire.* New York: Random House, 1945.

Mayhall, Mildred. *The Kiowas.* Norman: University of Oklahoma Press, 1971.

Miner, Craig, and William E. Unrau. *The End of Indian Kansas: A Study of Cultural Revolution, 1854–1871.* Lawrence: University of Kansas Press, 1990.

Morgan, Dale L. *Jedediah Smith and the Opening of the West.* Lincoln: University of Nebraska Press, 1964.

Morgan, Phyllis S. *Marc Simmons of New Mexico.* Albuquerque: University of New Mexico Press, 2005.

Moorhead, Max L. *New Mexico's Royal Road: Trade and Travel on the Chihuahua Trail.* Norman: University of Oklahoma Press, 1958.

Newcombe, W. W. Jr. *The Indians of Texas: From Prehistoric Times to the Present.* Austin: University of Texas Press, 1961.

Oliva, Leo E., ed. *Adventures on the Santa Fe Trail.* Topeka, Kans.: Kansas State Historical Society, 1988.

———. *Fort Dodge.* Topeka, Kans.: Kansas State Historical Society, 1998.

———. *Fort Hays.* Topeka, Kans.: Kansas State Historical Society, 1980.

———. *Fort Larned.* Topeka, Kans.: Kansas State Historical Society, 1982.

———. *Fort Scott.* Topeka, Kans.: Kansas State Historical Society, 1984.

———. *Fort Wallace.* Topeka, Kans.: Kansas State Historical Society, 1982.

———. *Soldiers on the Santa Fe Trail.* Norman: University of Oklahoma Press, 1967.

Ortiz, Simon J. *From Sand Creek.* Tucson: University of Arizona Press, 1981.

Poling-Kempes, Lesley. *The Harvey Girls: The Women Who Opened the West.* New York: Marlowe and Company, 1991.

Reddig, William M. *Tom's Town: Kansas City and the Pendergast Legend.* Philadelphia: Lippincott, 1947.

Roberts, David. *A Newer World: Kit Carson, John C. Fremont, and the Claiming of the American West.* New York: Simon and Schuster, 2000.

Ruxton, George Frederick. *Life in the Far West.* Norman: University of Oklahoma Press, 1951.

————. *Ruxton of the Rockies.* Collected by Clyde and Mae Reed Porter. Norman: University of Oklahoma Press, 1950.

Rollings, Willard H. *The Comanche.* New York: Chelsea House Publishers, 1989.

————. *The Osage: An Ethnohistorical Study of Hegemony on the Prairie Indians.* Columbia: University of Missouri, 1992.

Russell, Marian. *Land of Enchantment: Memoirs of Marian Russell along the Santa Fe Trail.* Evanston, Ill.: The Branding Iron Press, 1954.

Sanchez, Joseph P. *The Rio Abato Frontier: 1540–1690.* Albuquerque, N.Mex.: The Albuquerque Museum, 1987.

Sibley, George C. *The Road to Santa Fe: The Journal and Diary of George Champlin Sibley.* Edited by Kate Gregg. Albuquerque: University of New Mexico, 1995.

Simmons, Marc. *The Last Conquistador: Juan de Oñate and the Settling of the Far Southwest.* Norman: University of Oklahoma Press, 1991.

————. *New Mexico: An Interpretive History.* Albuquerque: University of New Mexico, 1988.

————. *The Old Santa Fe Trail: Collected Essays.* Albuquerque: University of New Mexico, 1996.

————, ed. *On the Santa Fe Trail.* Lawrence: University of Kansas Press, 1986.

————. *Spanish Pathways: Readings in the History of Hispanic New Mexico.* Albuquerque: University of New Mexico, 2001.

Simmons, Marc, and R. C. Gordon McCutchan. *The Short Truth about Kit Carson and the Indians.* Taos, N.Mex.: Kit Carson Historic Museum, 1993.

Simmons, Marc, and Hal Jackson. *Following the Santa Fe Trail: A Guide for Modern Travelers.* Santa Fe, N.Mex.: Ancient City Press, 2001.

Socolofsky, Homer E., and Huber Self. *Historical Atlas of Kansas.* Norman: University of Oklahoma Press, 1988.

Stocking, Hobart E. *The Road to Santa Fe.* New York: Hastings House Publishers, 1971.

Strom, Charles R. *Charles G. Parker: Wagonmaster on the Trail to Santa Fe.* White City, Kans.: Village Press, 1999.

Thomas, Diane. *The Southwest Indian Detours: The Story of Fred Harvey/Santa Fe Railway Experiment in Detourism.* Phoenix, Ariz.: Hunter Publishing, 1978.

Thomasma, Kenneth. *The Truth about Sacajawea.* Jackson, Wyo.: Grandview Publishing, 1997.

Tiller, Veronica E. Valverde. *The Jicarilla Apache Tribe: A History.* Albuquerque, N.Mex.: BowArrow Publishing Company, 2000.

Unrau, William E. *Indians of Kansas.* Topeka, Kans.: Kansas State Historical Society, 1991.

————. *The Kansa Indiana: A History of the Wind People, 1673–1873.* Norman: University of Oklahoma Press, 1971.

Wallace, Ernest, and E. Adamson Hoebel. *The Comanches: Lords of the Southern Plains.* Norman: University of Oklahoma Press, 1986.

Weber, David J. *The Spanish Frontier in North America.* New Haven, Conn.: Yale University Press, 1992.

Wedel, Waldo R. *An Introduction to Kansas Archeology.* Washington, D.C.: U.S. Government Printing Office, 1959.

Wolferman, Kristie C. *The Osage in Missouri.* Columbia: University of Missouri Press, 1997.

Zornow, William Frank. *Kansas: A History of the Jayhawk State.* Norman: University of Oklahoma Press, 1957.

INDEX

ABOUT THE AUTHOR

Steve Glassman is the author or editor of about 10 published books, including two novels and a travel narrative following in the footsteps of the man who discovered the civilization of the ancient Maya, John Lloyd Stephens. Many of his books are about Florida, several of which key on crime fiction. He has been nominated for an Edgar Alan Poe Award and was a Fulbright scholar/lecturer in Belize. He has twice been president of the Florida College English Association. He is a professor of humanities and communication at Embry-Riddle Aeronautical University in Daytona Beach.